Algorithms Illuminated
Part 3: Greedy Algorithms and Dynamic Programming

Tim Roughgarden

First Edition

Cover image: *Untitled*, by Johanna Dickson

ISBN: 978-0-9992829-4-6 (Paperback)
ISBN: 978-0-9992829-5-3 (ebook)

Library of Congress Control Number: 2017914282

Soundlikeyourself Publishing, LLC
New York, NY
soundlikeyourselfpublishing@gmail.com
www.algorithmsilluminated.org

In memory of
Stephen H. Schneider

Contents

Preface

This book is the third of a four-part series based on my online algorithms courses that have been running regularly since 2012, which in turn are based on an undergraduate course that I taught many times at Stanford University. The first two parts of the series are not strict prerequisites for this one, though portions of this book do assume at least a vague recollection of big-O notation (covered in Chapter 2 of *Part 1* or Appendix C of *Part 2*), divide-and-conquer algorithms (Chapter 3 of *Part 1*), and graphs (Chapter 7 of *Part 2*).

What We'll Cover

Algorithms Illuminated, Part 3 provides an introduction to and numerous case studies of two fundamental algorithm design paradigms.

Greedy algorithms and applications. Greedy algorithms solve problems by making a sequence of myopic and irrevocable decisions. For many problems, they are easy to devise and often blazingly fast. Most greedy algorithms are not guaranteed to be correct, but we'll cover several killer applications that are exceptions to this rule. Examples include scheduling problems, optimal compression, and minimum spanning trees of graphs.

Dynamic programming and applications. Few benefits of a serious study of algorithms rival the empowerment that comes from mastering dynamic programming. This design paradigm takes a lot of practice to perfect, but it has countless applications to problems that appear unsolvable using any simpler method. Our dynamic programming boot camp will double as a tour of some of the paradigm's killer applications, including the knapsack problem, the Needleman-Wunsch genome sequence alignment algorithm, Knuth's algorithm for optimal binary search trees, and the Bellman-Ford and Floyd-Warshall shortest-path algorithms.

For a more detailed look into the book's contents, check out the "Upshot" sections that conclude each chapter and highlight the most important points. The "Field Guide to Algorithm Design" on page 201 provides a bird's-eye view of how greedy algorithms and dynamic programming fit into the bigger algorithmic picture.

The starred sections of the book are the most advanced ones. The time-constrained reader can skip these sections on a first reading without any loss of continuity.

Topics covered in the other three parts. *Algorithms Illuminated, Part 1* covers asymptotic notation (big-O notation and its close cousins), divide-and-conquer algorithms and the master method, randomized QuickSort and its analysis, and linear-time selection algorithms. *Part 2* covers data structures (heaps, balanced search trees, hash tables, bloom filters), graph primitives (breadth- and depth-first search, connectivity, shortest paths), and their applications (ranging from deduplication to social network analysis). *Part 4* is all about NP-completeness, what it means for the algorithm designer, and strategies for coping with computationally intractable problems, including the analysis of heuristics and local search.

Skills You'll Learn

Mastering algorithms takes time and effort. Why bother?

Become a better programmer. You'll learn several blazingly fast subroutines for processing data as well as several useful data structures for organizing data that you can deploy directly in your own programs. Implementing and using these algorithms will stretch and improve your programming skills. You'll also learn general algorithm design paradigms that are relevant to many different problems across different domains, as well as tools for predicting the performance of such algorithms. These "algorithmic design patterns" can help you come up with new algorithms for problems that arise in your own work.

Sharpen your analytical skills. You'll get lots of practice describing and reasoning about algorithms. Through mathematical analysis, you'll gain a deep understanding of the specific algorithms and data structures that these books cover. You'll acquire facility with several mathematical techniques that are broadly useful for analyzing algorithms.

Think algorithmically. After you learn about algorithms, you'll start seeing them everywhere, whether you're riding an elevator, watching a flock of birds, managing your investment portfolio, or even watching an infant learn. Algorithmic thinking is increasingly useful and prevalent in disciplines outside of computer science, including biology, statistics, and economics.

Literacy with computer science's greatest hits. Studying algorithms can feel like watching a highlight reel of many of the greatest hits from the last sixty years of computer science. No longer will you feel excluded at that computer science cocktail party when someone cracks a joke about Dijkstra's algorithm. After reading these books, you'll know exactly what they mean.

Ace your technical interviews. Over the years, countless students have regaled me with stories about how mastering the concepts in these books enabled them to ace every technical interview question they were ever asked.

How These Books Are Different

This series of books has only one goal: *to teach the basics of algorithms in the most accessible way possible.* Think of them as a transcript of what an expert algorithms tutor would say to you over a series of one-on-one lessons.

There are a number of excellent more traditional and encyclopedic textbooks about algorithms, any of which usefully complement this book series with additional details, problems, and topics. I encourage you to explore and find your own favorites. There are also several books that, unlike these books, cater to programmers looking for ready-made algorithm implementations in a specific programming language. Many such implementations are freely available on the Web as well.

Who Are You?

The whole point of these books and the online courses upon which they are based is to be as widely and easily accessible as possible. People of all ages, backgrounds, and walks of life are well represented in my online courses, and there are large numbers of students (high-school, college, etc.), software engineers (both current and aspiring), scientists, and professionals hailing from all corners of the world.

This book is not an introduction to programming, and ideally you've acquired basic programming skills in a standard language (like Java, Python, C, Scala, Haskell, etc.). If you need to beef up your programming skills, there are several outstanding free online courses that teach basic programming.

We also use mathematical analysis as needed to understand how and why algorithms really work. The freely available book *Mathematics for Computer Science*, by Eric Lehman, F. Thomson Leighton, and Albert R. Meyer, is an excellent and entertaining refresher on mathematical notation (like $\sum$ and $\forall$), the basics of proofs (induction, contradiction, etc.), discrete probability, and much more.

Additional Resources

These books are based on online courses that are currently running on the Coursera and Stanford Lagunita platforms. I've made several resources available to help you replicate as much of the online course experience as you like.

Videos. If you're more in the mood to watch and listen than to read, check out the YouTube video playlists available from www.algorithmsilluminated.org. These videos cover all the topics in this book series, as well as additional advanced topics. I hope they exude a contagious enthusiasm for algorithms that, alas, is impossible to replicate fully on the printed page.

Quizzes. How can you know if you're truly absorbing the concepts in this book? Quizzes with solutions and explanations are scattered throughout the text; when you encounter one, I encourage you to pause and think about the answer before reading on.

End-of-chapter problems. At the end of each chapter you'll find several relatively straightforward questions for testing your understanding, followed by harder and more open-ended challenge problems. Hints or solutions to all of these problems (as indicated by an "*(H)*" or "*(S)*," respectively) are included at the end of the book. Readers can interact with me and each other about the end-of-chapter problems through the book's discussion forum (see below).

Programming problems. Each of the chapters concludes with a suggested programming project whose goal is to help you develop a detailed understanding of an algorithm by creating your own working implementation of it. Data sets, along with test cases and their solutions, can be found at `www.algorithmsilluminated.org`.

Discussion forums. A big reason for the success of online courses is the opportunities they provide for participants to help each other understand the course material and debug programs through discussion forums. Readers of these books have the same opportunity, via the forums available at `www.algorithmsilluminated.org`.

Acknowledgments

These books would not exist without the passion and hunger supplied by the hundreds of thousands of participants in my algorithms courses over the years. I am particularly grateful to those who supplied detailed feedback on an earlier draft of this book: Tonya Blust, Yuan Cao, Carlos Guia, Jim Humelsine, Vladimir Kokshenev, Bayram Kuliyev, and Daniel Zingaro.

I always appreciate suggestions and corrections from readers. These are best communicated through the discussion forums mentioned above.

Tim Roughgarden
New York, NY
April 2019

Chapter 13

Introduction to Greedy Algorithms

Much of the beauty in the design and analysis of algorithms stems from the interplay between general algorithm design principles and the instantiation of these principles to solve concrete computational problems. There's no silver bullet in algorithm design—no universal technique that can solve every computational problem you'll encounter. But there *are* several general design paradigms that can help you solve problems from many different application domains. Teaching you these paradigms and their most famous instantiations is one of the major goals of this book series.

13.1 The Greedy Algorithm Design Paradigm

13.1.1 Algorithm Paradigms

What's an "algorithm design paradigm?" Readers of *Part 1* have already seen a canonical example, the divide-and-conquer paradigm. That paradigm went like this:

The Divide-and-Conquer Paradigm

1. *Divide* the input into smaller subproblems.

2. *Conquer* the subproblems recursively.

3. *Combine* the solutions for the subproblems into a solution for the original problem.

In *Part 1* we saw numerous instantiations of this paradigm: the MergeSort and QuickSort algorithms, Karatsuba's $O(n^{1.59})$-time algorithm for multiplying two n-digit integers, Strassen's $O(n^{2.71})$-time algorithm for multiplying two $n \times n$ matrices, and more.

1

The first half of this book is about the *greedy* algorithm design paradigm. What is a greedy algorithm, exactly? Much blood and ink have been spilled over this question, so we'll content ourselves with an informal definition.[1]

The Greedy Paradigm

Construct a solution iteratively, via a sequence of myopic decisions, and hope that everything works out in the end.

The best way to get a feel for greedy algorithms is through examples. We'll see several over the next few chapters.[2]

13.1.2   Themes of the Greedy Paradigm

Here are a few themes to watch for in our examples. (You might want to re-read this section after going through one or more examples, so that it's less abstract.) First, for many problems, it's surprisingly easy to come up with one or even multiple greedy algorithms that might plausibly work. This is both a bug and a feature—greedy algorithms can be a great cure for writer's block when you're stuck on a problem, but it can be hard to assess which greedy approach is the most promising. Second, the running time analysis is often a one-liner. For example, many greedy algorithms boil down to sorting plus a linear amount of extra processing, in which case the running time of a good implementation would be $O(n \log n)$, where n is the number of objects to be sorted.[3] (Big-O notation suppresses constant

---

[1]To investigate formal definitions of greedy algorithms, start with the paper "(Incremental) Priority Algorithms," by Allan Borodin, Morten N. Nielsen, and Charles Rackoff (*Algorithmica*, 2003).

[2]Readers of *Part 2* have already seen a greedy algorithm, namely Dijkstra's shortest-path algorithm. That algorithm iteratively computes the shortest-path distances from a starting vertex s to every other vertex of a graph. In each iteration, the algorithm irrevocably and myopically commits to an estimate of the shortest-path distance to one additional vertex, never revisiting the decision. In graphs with only nonnegative edge lengths, everything works out in the end and all the shortest-path distance estimates are correct.

[3]For example, two $O(n \log n)$-time sorting algorithms are MergeSort (see Chapter 1 in *Part 1*) and HeapSort (see Chapter 10 in *Part 2*). Alternatively, randomized QuickSort (see Chapter 5 of *Part 1*) has an average running time of $O(n \log n)$.

factors and different logarithmic functions differ by a constant factor, so there is no need to specify the base of the logarithm.) Finally, it's often difficult to figure out whether a proposed greedy algorithm actually returns the correct output for every possible input. The fear is that one of the algorithm's irrevocable myopic decisions will come back to haunt you and, with full hindsight, be revealed as a terrible idea. And even when a greedy algorithm *is* correct, proving it can be difficult.[4]

Features and Bugs of the Greedy Paradigm

1. Easy to come up with one or more greedy algorithms.

2. Easy to analyze the running time.

3. Hard to establish correctness.

One of the reasons why it can be hard to prove the correctness of greedy algorithms is that most such algorithms are *not* correct, meaning there exist inputs for which the algorithm fails to produce the desired output. If you remember only one thing about greedy algorithms, it should be this.

Warning

Most greedy algorithms are not always correct.

This point is especially difficult to accept for clever greedy algorithms that you invented yourself. You might believe, in your heart of hearts, that your natural greedy algorithm must always solve the problem correctly. More often than not, this belief is unfounded.[5]

---

[4]Veterans of *Part 1* know that all three themes are a big contrast to the divide-and-conquer paradigm. It's often tricky to come up with a good divide-and-conquer algorithm for a problem, and when you do, there's usually a "Eureka!" moment when you know that you've cracked the problem. Analyzing the running times of divide-and-conquer algorithms can be difficult, due to the tug-of-war between the forces of proliferating subproblems and shrinking work-per-subproblem. (All of Chapter 4 of *Part 1* is devoted to this topic.) Finally, proofs of correctness for divide-and-conquer algorithms are usually straightforward inductions.

[5]A not-always-correct greedy algorithm can still serve as a super-fast heuristic for a problem, a point we'll return to in *Part 4*.

Now that my conscience is clear, let's look at some cherry-picked examples of problems that *can* be solved correctly with a judiciously designed greedy algorithm.

13.2 A Scheduling Problem

Our first case study concerns *scheduling*, in which the goal is to schedule tasks on one or more shared resources to optimize some objective. For example, a resource could represent a computer processor (with tasks corresponding to jobs), a classroom (with tasks corresponding to lectures), or your calendar for the day (with tasks corresponding to meetings).

13.2.1 The Setup

In scheduling, the tasks to be completed are usually called *jobs*, and jobs can have different characteristics. Suppose that each job j has a known *length* ℓ_j, which is the amount of time required to process the job (for example, the length of a lecture or meeting). Also, each job has a *weight* w_j, with higher weights corresponding to higher-priority jobs.

13.2.2 Completion Times

A *schedule* specifies an order in which to process the jobs. In a problem instance with n jobs, there are $n! = n \cdot (n-1) \cdot (n-2) \cdots 2 \cdot 1$ different schedules. That's a lot of schedules! Which one should we prefer?

Next, we need to define an *objective function* that assigns a numerical score to every schedule and quantifies what we want. First, a preliminary definition:

Completion Times

The *completion time* $C_j(\sigma)$ of a job j in a schedule σ is the sum of the lengths of the jobs preceding j in σ, plus the length of j itself.

In other words, a job's completion time in a schedule is the total time that elapses before the job has been fully processed.

Quiz 13.1

Consider a problem instance that has three jobs with $\ell_1 = 1$, $\ell_2 = 2$, and $\ell_3 = 3$, and suppose they are scheduled in this order (with job 1 first). What are the completion times of the three jobs in this schedule? (The job weights are irrelevant for this question, so we have not specified them.)

a) 1, 2, and 3

b) 3, 5, and 6

c) 1, 3, and 6

d) 1, 4, and 6

(See Section 13.2.4 for the solution and discussion.)

13.2.3   Objective Function

What makes for a good schedule? We'd like jobs' completion times to be small, but trade-offs between jobs are inevitable—in any schedule, jobs scheduled early will have short completion times while those scheduled toward the end will have long completion times.

One way to make trade-offs between the jobs is to minimize the *sum of weighted completion times*. In math, this objective function translates to

$$\min_{\sigma} \sum_{j=1}^{n} w_j C_j(\sigma), \qquad (13.1)$$

where the minimization is over all $n!$ possible schedules σ, and $C_j(\sigma)$ denotes job j's completion time in the schedule σ. This is equivalent to minimizing the weighted average of the jobs' completion times, with the averaging weights proportional to the w_j's.

For example, consider the three jobs in Quiz 13.1 and suppose their weights are $w_1 = 3$, $w_2 = 2$, and $w_3 = 1$. If we schedule the first job first, the second job second, and the third job third, the sum of the weighted completion times is

$$\underbrace{3 \cdot 1}_{\text{job } \#1} + \underbrace{2 \cdot 3}_{\text{job } \#2} + \underbrace{1 \cdot 6}_{\text{job } \#3} = 15.$$

By checking all 3! = 6 possible schedules, you can verify that this is the schedule that minimizes the sum of weighted completion times. How can we solve this problem in general, given as input an arbitrary set of job lengths and weights?

Problem: Minimizing the Sum of Weighted Completion Times

Input: A set of n jobs with positive lengths $\ell_1, \ell_2, \ldots, \ell_n$ and positive weights $w_1, w_2, \ldots, w_n$.

Output: A job sequence that minimizes the sum of weighted completion times (13.1).

With $n!$ different schedules, computing the best one by exhaustive search is out of the question for all but the tiniest instances. We need a smarter algorithm.[6]

13.2.4   Solution to Quiz 13.1

Correct answer: (c). We can visualize a schedule by stacking the jobs on top of one another, with time increasing from bottom to top (Figure 13.1). The completion time of a job is the time corresponding to its topmost edge. For the first job, its completion time is just its length, which is 1. The second job must wait for the first job to complete, so its completion time is the sum of the lengths of the first two jobs, which is 3. The third job doesn't even start until time 3, and then it takes 3 more time units to complete, so its completion time is 6.

13.3   Developing a Greedy Algorithm

Greedy algorithms seem like a good fit for the problem of scheduling jobs to minimize the weighted sum of completion times. The output has an iterative structure, with jobs processed one by one. Why not

---

[6]For example, $n!$ is bigger than 3.6 million when $n = 10$, bigger than 2.4 quintillion when $n = 20$, and bigger than the estimated number of atoms in the known universe when $n \geq 60$. Thus no conceivable improvement in computer technology would transmute exhaustive search into a useful algorithm.

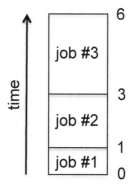

Figure 13.1: The completion times of the three jobs are 1, 3, and 6.

use a greedy algorithm that iteratively decides which job should go next?

The first step of our plan is to solve two special cases of the general problem. Our solutions to these will suggest what a greedy algorithm might look like in the general case. We'll then narrow the field to a single candidate algorithm and prove that this candidate correctly solves the problem. The process by which we arrive at this algorithm is more important to remember than the algorithm itself; it's a repeatable process that you can use in your own applications.

13.3.1   Two Special Cases

Let's think positive and posit that there actually is a correct greedy algorithm for the problem of minimizing the weighted sum of completion times. What would it look like? For starters, what if you knew that all the jobs had the same length (but possibly different weights)? What if they all had the same weight (but possibly different lengths)?

Quiz 13.2

(1) If all job lengths are identical, should we schedule smaller- or larger-weight jobs earlier?

(2) If all job weights are identical, should we schedule shorter or longer jobs earlier?

---

a) larger/shorter

b) smaller/shorter

c) larger/longer

d) smaller/longer

(See Section 13.3.3 for the solution and discussion.)

13.3.2 Dueling Greedy Algorithms

In the general case, jobs can have different weights and different lengths. Whenever our two rules-of-thumb—to prefer shorter jobs and higher-weight jobs—luckily coincide for a pair of jobs, we know which one to schedule first (the shorter, higher-weight one). But what if the two rules give conflicting advice? What should we do with one short low-weight job and one long high-weight job?

What's the simplest greedy algorithm that might work? Each job has two parameters, and the algorithm must look at both. The best-case scenario would be to come up with a formula that compiles each job's length and weight into a single *score*, so that scheduling jobs from highest to lowest score is guaranteed to minimize the sum of weighted completion times. If such a formula exists, our two special cases imply that it must have two properties: (i) holding the length fixed, it should be increasing in the job's weight; and (ii) holding the weight fixed, it should be decreasing in the job's length. (Remember, higher scores are better.) Take a minute to brainstorm some formulas that have both of these properties.

* * * * * * * * * * *

Perhaps the simplest function that is increasing in weight and decreasing in length is the difference between the two:

proposal #1 for score of job j: $w_j - \ell_j$.

This score might be negative, but that poses no obstacle to sequencing the jobs from highest to lowest score.

There are plenty of other options. For example, the ratio of the two parameters is another candidate:

proposal #2 for score of job j: $\dfrac{w_j}{\ell_j}$.

These two scoring functions lead to two different greedy algorithms.

GreedyDiff

Schedule the jobs in decreasing order of $w_j - \ell_j$
(breaking ties arbitrarily).

GreedyRatio

Schedule the jobs in decreasing order of $\dfrac{w_j}{\ell_j}$
(breaking ties arbitrarily).

Thus, already, our first case study illustrates the first theme of the greedy paradigm (Section 13.1.2): It is often easy to propose multiple competing greedy algorithms for a problem.

Which of the two algorithms, if any, is correct? A quick way to rule out one of them is to find an instance in which the two algorithms output different schedules, with different objective function values. For whichever algorithm fares worse in this example, we can conclude that it is not always optimal.

Both algorithms do the right thing in our two special cases, with equal-weight or equal-length jobs. The simplest possible example for ruling out one of them would be a problem instance with two jobs, having different weights and lengths, such that the two algorithms schedule the jobs in opposite orders. That is, we seek two jobs whose ordering by difference is the opposite of their ordering by ratio. One simple example is:

	Job #1	Job #2
Length	$\ell_1 = 5$	$\ell_2 = 2$
Weight	$w_1 = 3$	$w_2 = 1.$

The first job has the larger ratio ($\frac{3}{5}$ vs. $\frac{1}{2}$) but the smaller (more negative) difference (-2 vs. -1). Thus the GreedyDiff algorithm schedules the second job first, while GreedyRatio does the opposite.

Quiz 13.3

What is the sum of weighted completion times in the schedules output by the GreedyDiff and GreedyRatio algorithms, respectively?

a) 22 and 23

b) 23 and 22

c) 17 and 17

d) 17 and 11

(See Section 13.3.3 for the solution and discussion.)

We've made progress by ruling out the GreedyDiff algorithm from further consideration. However, the outcome of Quiz 13.3 does *not* immediately imply that the GreedyRatio algorithm is always optimal. For all we know, there are other cases in which the algorithm outputs a suboptimal schedule. You should always be skeptical about an algorithm that does not come with a proof of correctness, even if the algorithm does the right thing in some toy examples, and extra-skeptical of greedy algorithms.

In our case, the GreedyRatio algorithm *is*, in fact, guaranteed to minimize the sum of weighted completion times.

Theorem 13.1 (Correctness of GreedyRatio) *For every set of positive job weights* $w_1, w_2, \ldots, w_n$ *and positive job lengths* $\ell_1, \ell_2, \ldots, \ell_n$, *the GreedyRatio algorithm outputs a schedule with the minimum-possible sum of weighted completion times.*

This assertion is not obvious and you should not trust it until I supply you with a proof. Consistent with the third theme of the greedy paradigm (Section 13.1.2), this proof occupies the entire next section.

On Lemmas, Theorems, and the Like

In mathematical writing, the most important technical statements are labeled *theorems*. A *lemma* is a technical statement that assists with the proof of a theorem (much as a subroutine assists with the implementation of a larger program). A *corollary* is a statement that follows immediately from an already-proven result, such as a special case of a theorem. We use the term *proposition* for stand-alone technical statements that are not particularly important in their own right.

The remaining theme of the greedy paradigm is the ease of running time analyses (Section 13.1.2). That's certainly the case here. All the `GreedyRatio` algorithm does is sort the jobs by ratio, which requires $O(n \log n)$ time, where n is the number of jobs in the input (see footnote 3).

13.3.3   Solutions to Quiz 13.2–13.3

Solution to Quiz 13.2

Correct answer: (a). First suppose that all n jobs have the same length, say length 1. Then, every schedule has exactly the same set of completion times—$\{1, 2, 3, \ldots, n\}$—and the only question is which job gets which completion time. Our semantics for job weights certainly suggests that the higher-weight jobs should receive the smaller completion times, and this is in fact the case. For example, you wouldn't want to schedule a job with weight 10 third (with completion time 3) and one with weight 20 fifth (with completion time 5); you'd be better off exchanging the positions of these two jobs, which would decrease the sum of weighted completion times by 20 (as you should check).

The second case, in which all jobs have equal weights, is a little more subtle. Here, you want to favor shorter jobs. For example, consider two unit-weight jobs with lengths 1 and 2. If you schedule the shorter job first, the completion times are 1 and 3, for a total of 4. In the opposite order, the completion times are 2 and 3, for an inferior total of 5. In general, the job scheduled first contributes to the completion times of *all* the jobs, as all jobs must wait for the first one to finish. All else being equal, scheduling the shortest job first minimizes this negative impact. The second job contributes to all the completion times other than that of the first job, so the second-shortest job should be scheduled next, and so on.

Solution to Quiz 13.3

Correct answer: (b). The `GreedyDiff` algorithm schedules the second job first. The completion time of this job is $C_2 = \ell_2 = 2$ while that of the other job is $C_1 = \ell_2 + \ell_1 = 7$. The sum of weighted completion times is then

$$w_1 \cdot C_1 + w_2 \cdot C_2 = 3 \cdot 7 + 1 \cdot 2 = 23.$$

The `GreedyRatio` algorithm schedules the first job first, resulting in completion times $C_1 = \ell_1 = 5$ and $C_2 = \ell_1 + \ell_2 = 7$ and a sum of weighted completion times of

$$3 \cdot 5 + 1 \cdot 7 = 22.$$

We conclude that the `GreedyDiff` algorithm fails to compute an optimal schedule for this example and therefore is not always correct.

13.4 Proof of Correctness

Divide-and-conquer algorithms usually have formulaic correctness proofs, consisting of a straightforward induction. Not so with greedy algorithms, for which correctness proofs are more art than science—be prepared to throw in the kitchen sink. To the extent that there are recurring themes in correctness proofs of greedy algorithms, we will emphasize them as we go along.

The proof of Theorem 13.1 includes a vivid example of one such theme: *exchange arguments*. The key idea is to prove that every feasible solution can be improved by modifying it to look more like the output of the greedy algorithm. We'll see two variants in this section. In the first, we'll proceed by contradiction and use an exchange argument to exhibit a "too-good-to-be-true" solution. In the second, we'll use an exchange argument to show that every feasible solution can be iteratively massaged into the output of the greedy algorithm, while only improving the solution along the way.[7]

13.4.1   The No-Ties Case: High-Level Plan

We proceed to the proof of Theorem 13.1. Fix a set of jobs, with positive weights $w_1, w_2, \ldots, w_n$ and lengths $\ell_1, \ell_2 \ldots, \ell_n$. We must show that the GreedyRatio algorithm produces a schedule that minimizes the sum of weighted completion times (13.1). We start with two assumptions.

Two Assumptions

(1) The jobs are indexed in nonincreasing order of weight-length ratio:

$$\frac{w_1}{\ell_1} \geq \frac{w_2}{\ell_2} \geq \cdots \geq \frac{w_n}{\ell_n}. \qquad (13.2)$$

(2) There are no ties between ratios: $\frac{w_i}{\ell_i} \neq \frac{w_j}{\ell_j}$ whenever $i \neq j$.

The first assumption is without loss of generality, merely an agreement among friends to minimize our notational burden. Reordering the jobs in the input has no effect on the problem to be solved. We can therefore always reorder and reindex the jobs so that (13.2) holds. The second assumption imposes a non-trivial restriction on the input; we will do some extra work to remove it in Section 13.4.4. Together, the two assumptions imply that jobs are indexed in strictly decreasing order of weight-length ratio.

The high-level plan is to proceed by contradiction. Recall that in this type of proof, you assume the *opposite* of what you want to prove, and then build on this assumption with a sequence of logically correct steps that culminates in a patently false statement. Such a

---

[7]Exchange arguments are only one way among many to prove that a greedy algorithm is correct. For example, in Chapter 9 of *Part 2*, our correctness proof for Dijkstra's algorithm used induction rather than an exchange argument. Both induction and exchange arguments play a role in our correctness proofs for Huffman's greedy coding algorithm (Chapter 14) and for Prim's and Kruskal's minimum spanning tree algorithms (Chapter 15).

contradiction implies that the assumption can't be true, which proves the desired statement.

To begin, we assume that the GreedyRatio algorithm produces a schedule σ of the given jobs that is *not* optimal. Thus, there is an optimal schedule σ^* of these jobs with a strictly smaller sum of weighted completion times. The inspired idea is to use the differences between σ and σ^* to explicitly construct a schedule that is *even better than σ^**; this will contradict our assumption that σ^* is an optimal schedule.

13.4.2   Exchanging Jobs in a Consecutive Inversion

Suppose, for contradiction, that the GreedyRatio algorithm produces the schedule σ and that there is an optimal schedule σ^* with a strictly smaller sum of weighted completion times. By assumption (1), the greedy schedule σ schedules the jobs in order of index (with job 1 first, then job 2, all the way up to job n); see Figure 13.2.

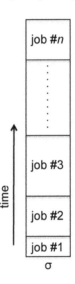

Figure 13.2: The greedy schedule σ, with jobs scheduled in order of nonincreasing weight-length ratio.

Going from bottom to top in the greedy schedule, the indices of the jobs always go up. This is not true for any other schedule. To make this assertion precise, define a *consecutive inversion* in a schedule as a pair i, j of jobs such that $i > j$ and job i is processed immediately before job j. For example, in Figure 13.2, if jobs 2 and 3 were processed in the opposite order they would constitute a consecutive inversion (with $i = 3$ and $j = 2$).

Lemma 13.2 (Non-Greedy Schedules Have Inversions)
Every schedule $\hat{\sigma}$ different from the greedy schedule σ has at least one consecutive inversion.

Proof: We prove the contrapositive.[8] If $\hat{\sigma}$ has no consecutive inversions, the index of each job is at least 1 larger than the job that came before it. There are n jobs and the maximum-possible index is n, so there cannot be any jumps of 2 or more between the indices of consecutive jobs. This means that $\hat{\sigma}$ is the same as the schedule computed by the greedy algorithm. *QED*[9]

Returning to the proof of Theorem 13.1, we are assuming that there is an optimal schedule σ^* of the given jobs with a strictly smaller sum of weighted completion times than the greedy schedule σ. Because $\sigma^* \neq \sigma$, Lemma 13.2 applies to σ^*, and there are consecutive jobs i, j in σ^* with $i > j$ (Figure 13.3(a)). How can we use this fact to exhibit another schedule σ' that is even better than σ^*, thereby furnishing a contradiction?

The key idea is to perform an *exchange*. We define a new schedule σ' that is identical to σ^* except that the jobs i and j are processed in the opposite order, with j now processed immediately before i. The jobs before both i and j ("stuff" in Figure 13.3) are the same in both σ^* and σ' (and in the same order), and likewise for the jobs that follow both i and j ("more stuff").

13.4.3   Cost-Benefit Analysis

What are the ramifications of the exchange illustrated below in Figure 13.3?

---

[8]The *contrapositive* of a statement "if A is true, then B is true" is the logically equivalent statement "if B is not true, then A is not true." For example, the contrapositive of Lemma 13.2 is: If $\hat{\sigma}$ has no consecutive inversions, then $\hat{\sigma}$ is the same as the greedy schedule σ.

[9]"Q.e.d." is an abbreviation for *quod erat demonstrandum* and means "that which was to be demonstrated." In mathematical writing, it is used at the end of a proof to mark its completion.

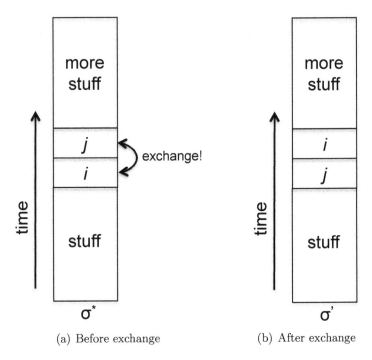

(a) Before exchange   (b) After exchange

Figure 13.3: Obtaining the new schedule σ' from the allegedly optimal schedule σ^* by exchanging the jobs in a consecutive inversion (with $i > j$).

Quiz 13.4

What effect does the exchange have on the completion time of: (i) a job other than i or j; (ii) the job i; and (iii) the job j?

a) (i) Not enough information to answer; (ii) goes up; (iii) goes down.

b) (i) Not enough information to answer; (ii) goes down; (iii) goes up.

c) (i) Unaffected; (ii) goes up; (iii) goes down.

d) (i) Unaffected; (ii) goes down; (iii) goes up.

(See Section 13.4.5 for the solution and discussion.)

Solving Quiz 13.4 puts us in a great position to finish the proof. The cost of exchanging the jobs i and j in a consecutive inversion is that i's completion time C_i goes up by the length ℓ_j of job j, which increases the objective function (13.1) by $w_i \cdot \ell_j$. The benefit is that j's completion time C_j goes down by the length ℓ_i of job i, which decreases the objective function (13.1) by $w_j \cdot \ell_i$. Summarizing,

$$\underbrace{\sum_{k=1}^{n} w_k C_k(\sigma')}_{\text{objective fn value of } \sigma'} = \underbrace{\sum_{k=1}^{n} w_k C_k(\sigma^*)}_{\text{objective fn value of } \sigma^*} + \underbrace{w_i \ell_j - w_j \ell_i}_{\text{effect of exchange}} . \quad (13.3)$$

Now is the time to use the fact that σ^* scheduled i and j in the "wrong order," with $i > j$. Our standing assumptions (1) and (2) imply that jobs are indexed in strictly decreasing order of weight-length ratio, so

$$\frac{w_i}{\ell_i} < \frac{w_j}{\ell_j}.$$

After clearing denominators, this translates to

$$\underbrace{w_i \ell_j}_{\text{cost of exchange}} < \underbrace{w_j \ell_i}_{\text{benefit of exchange}} .$$

Because the benefit of the exchange exceeds the cost, equation (13.3) tells us that

objective function value of $\sigma' <$ objective function value of σ^*.

But this is nuts—σ^* was supposed to be an optimal schedule, with the smallest possible sum of weighted completion times! We've arrived at the desired contradiction, which completes the proof of Theorem 13.1 for the case in which all the jobs have distinct weight-length ratios.

13.4.4   Handling Ties

With a little more work, we can prove the correctness of the GreedyRatio algorithm (Theorem 13.1) even when there are ties in jobs' weight-length ratios. (We'll keep the assumption (1) that jobs are indexed in nonincreasing order of weight-length ratio, as it's without loss of generality.) The point of going through this more general correctness proof is to illustrate a neat twist on the exchange argument from the previous section, which proceeds directly rather than by contradiction.

We'll reuse much of our previous work, but our high-level plan is different. As before, let $\sigma = 1, 2, \ldots, n$ denote the schedule computed by the GreedyRatio algorithm. Consider an arbitrary competing schedule σ^*, optimal or otherwise. We'll show directly, by a sequence of job exchanges, that σ's sum of weighted completion times is no larger than that of σ^*. Having proved this for every schedule σ^*, we'll conclude that σ is, in fact, an optimal schedule.

In more detail, assume that $\sigma^* \neq \sigma$. (There's nothing to do if $\sigma^* = \sigma$.) By Lemma 13.2, σ^* has a consecutive inversion—two jobs i and j such that $i > j$ and j is scheduled immediately after i. Obtain σ' from σ^* by swapping the positions of i and j in the schedule (Figure 13.3). As in our derivation of the equation (13.3), the cost and benefit of this exchange are $w_i \ell_j$ and $w_j \ell_i$, respectively. Because $i > j$ and jobs are indexed in nonincreasing order of weight-length ratio,

$$\frac{w_i}{\ell_i} \leq \frac{w_j}{\ell_j}$$

and hence

$$\underbrace{w_i \ell_j}_{\text{cost of exchange}} \leq \underbrace{w_j \ell_i}_{\text{benefit of exchange}} . \tag{13.4}$$

In other words, the swap cannot increase the sum of weighted completion times—the sum might decrease, or it might stay the same.[10]

Have we made any progress?

Quiz 13.5

An *inversion* in a schedule is a pair k, m of jobs with $k < m$ and m processed before k. (The jobs k and m need not be consecutive—some jobs might be scheduled after m and before k.) Suppose σ_1 is a schedule with a consecutive inversion i, j with $i > j$, and obtain σ_2 from σ_1 by reversing the order of i and j. How does the number of inversions in σ_2 compare to that in σ_1?

---

[10]We no longer get an immediate contradiction in the case in which σ^* is an optimal schedule, as σ' could be a different, equally optimal, schedule.

---

a) σ_2 has one fewer inversion than σ_1.

b) σ_2 has the same number of inversions as σ_1.

c) σ_2 has one more inversion than σ_1.

d) None of the other answers are correct.

(See Section 13.4.5 for the solution and discussion.)

To finish the proof, take the arbitrary competing schedule σ^* and repeatedly swap jobs to remove consecutive inversions.[11] Because the number of inversions decreases with every swap (Quiz 13.5), this process eventually terminates. By Lemma 13.2, it can only terminate at the greedy schedule σ. The objective function value can only decrease throughout this process (by (13.4)), so σ is at least as good as σ^*. This is true for every choice of σ^*, so σ is indeed optimal. $\mathcal{QED}$

13.4.5   Solution to Quizzes 13.4–13.5

Solution to Quiz 13.4

Correct answer: (c). First, jobs k other than i and j couldn't care less about i and j being swapped. This is easiest to see for a job k processed before i and j in σ^* (as part of the "stuff" in Figure 13.3). Because the exchange occurs after k completes, it has no effect on k's completion time (the amount of time that elapses before k completes). For a job k processed after i and j in σ^* (as part of the "more stuff" in Figure 13.3), the set of jobs completed before k is exactly the same in σ^* and in σ'. The completion time of a job depends only on the set of jobs preceding it (and not on their order), so job k is none the wiser and completes at the same time in both schedules.

As for job i, its completion time goes up in σ'. It must wait for the same jobs as before ("stuff"), and now job j as well, so its completion time increases by ℓ_j. Similarly, job j waits for the same jobs to complete as before, except that in σ' it no longer waits for i. Thus job j's completion time decreases by ℓ_i.

---

[11]Readers familiar with the BubbleSort algorithm might recognize its use here—though only in the analysis, not in the algorithm!

Solution to Quiz 13.5

Correct answer: (a). If $\{k, m\} = \{i, j\}$, then k and m form an inversion in σ_1 but not in σ_2 (because the swap un-inverts them). If at least one of k or m is different from both i and j, and hence appears either before both i and j or after both i and j in both schedules, the swap has no effect on the relative order of k and m (see Figure 13.4). We conclude that σ_2 has exactly the same inversions as σ_1, except with the inversion of i and j removed.

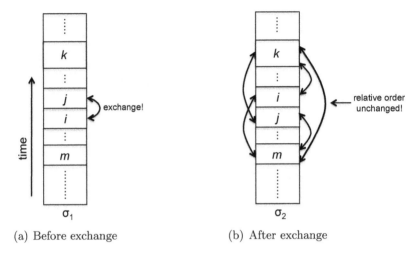

(a) Before exchange   (b) After exchange

Figure 13.4: Swapping jobs in a consecutive inversion decreases the total number of inversions by 1. The five highlighted pairs of jobs in (b) are in the same relative order in both schedules.

The Upshot

☆ Greedy algorithms construct solutions iteratively, via a sequence of myopic decisions, and hope that everything works out in the end.

☆ It is often easy to propose one or more greedy algorithms for a problem and to analyze their running times.

☆ Most greedy algorithms are not always correct.

★ Even when a greedy algorithm is always correct, proving it can be difficult.

★ Given tasks with lengths and weights, greedily ordering them from highest to lowest weight-length ratio minimizes the weighted sum of completion times.

★ Exchange arguments are among the most common techniques used in correctness proofs for greedy algorithms. The idea is to show that every feasible solution can be improved by modifying it to look more like the output of the greedy algorithm.

Test Your Understanding

Problem 13.1 *(H)* You are given as input n jobs, each with a length ℓ_j and a deadline d_j. Define the *lateness* $\lambda_j(\sigma)$ of a job j in a schedule σ as the difference $C_j(\sigma) - d_j$ between the job's completion time and deadline, or as 0 if $C_j(\sigma) \le d_j$. (See page 4 for the definition of a job's completion time in a schedule.) This problem considers the objective of minimizing the maximum lateness, $\max_{j=1}^{n} \lambda_j(\sigma)$.

Which of the following greedy algorithms produces a schedule that minimizes the maximum lateness? Feel free to assume that there are no ties.

a) Schedule the jobs in increasing order of deadline d_j.

b) Schedule the jobs in increasing order of processing time p_j.

c) Schedule the jobs in increasing order of the product $d_j \cdot p_j$.

d) None of the other answers are correct.

Problem 13.2 *(H)* Continuing Problem 13.1, consider instead the objective of minimizing the *total* lateness, $\sum_{j=1}^{n} \lambda_j(\sigma)$.

Which of the following greedy algorithms produces a schedule that minimizes the total lateness? Feel free to assume that there are no ties.

a) Schedule the jobs in increasing order of deadline d_j.

b) Schedule the jobs in increasing order of processing time p_j.

c) Schedule the jobs in increasing order of the product $d_j \cdot p_j$.

d) None of the other answers are correct.

Problem 13.3 *(H)* You are given as input n jobs, each with a start time s_j and a finish time t_j. Two jobs *conflict* if they overlap in time—if one of them starts between the start and finish times of the other. In this problem, the goal is to select a maximum-size subset of jobs that have no conflicts. (For example, given three jobs consuming the intervals $[0,3]$, $[2,5]$, and $[4,7]$, the optimal solution consists of the first and third jobs.) The plan is to design an iterative greedy algorithm that, in each iteration, irrevocably adds a new job j to the solution-so-far and removes from future consideration all jobs that conflict with j.

Which of the following greedy algorithms is guaranteed to compute an optimal solution? Feel free to assume that there are no ties.

a) At each iteration, choose the remaining job with the earliest finish time.

b) At each iteration, choose the remaining job with the earliest start time.

c) At each iteration, choose the remaining job that requires the least time (that is, with the smallest value of $t_j - s_j$).

d) At each iteration, choose the remaining job with the fewest number of conflicts with other remaining jobs.

Programming Problems

Problem 13.4 Implement in your favorite programming language the GreedyDiff and GreedyRatio algorithms from Section 13.3 for minimizing the weighted sum of completion times. Run both algorithms on several examples. How much better are the schedules computed by the GreedyRatio algorithm than those by the GreedyDiff algorithm? (See www.algorithmsilluminated.org for test cases and challenge data sets.)

Chapter 14

Huffman Codes

Everybody loves compression. The number of photos you can store on your smartphone? It depends on how much you can compress the files with little or no loss. The time required to download a file? The more you compress, the faster the download. *Huffman coding* is a widely-used method for lossless compression. For example, every time you import or export an MP3 audio file, your computer uses Huffman codes. In this chapter, we'll learn about the optimality of Huffman codes, as well as a blazingly fast greedy algorithm for computing them.

14.1 Codes

14.1.1 Fixed-Length Binary Codes

Let's set the stage before we proceed to a problem definition or algorithm. An *alphabet* Σ is a finite non-empty set of symbols. For example, Σ might be a set of 64 symbols that includes all 26 letters (both upper and lower case) plus punctuation and some special characters. A *binary code* for an alphabet is a way of writing each of its symbols as a distinct binary string (i.e., as a sequence of *bits*, meaning 0s and 1s).[1] For example, with an alphabet of 64 symbols, a natural encoding is to associate each symbol with one of the $2^6 = 64$ length-6 binary strings, with each string used exactly once. This is an example of a *fixed-length* binary code, which uses the same number of bits to encode each symbol. This is roughly how ASCII codes work, for instance.

Fixed-length codes are a natural solution, but we can't get complacent. As always, it's our duty to ask the question: *Can we do better?*

---

[1] The abbreviation "i.e." stands for *id est*, and means "that is."

14.1.2   Variable-Length Codes

When some symbols of the alphabet occur much more frequently than others, variable-length codes can be more efficient than fixed-length ones. Allowing variable-length codes introduces a complication, however, which we illustrate by example. Consider a four-symbol alphabet, say $\Sigma = \{A, B, C, D\}$. One natural fixed-length code for this alphabet is:

Symbol	Encoding
A	00
B	01
C	10
D	11

Suppose we wanted to get away with fewer bits in our code by using a 1-bit encoding for some of the symbols. For example, we could try:

Symbol	Encoding
A	0
B	01
C	10
D	1

This shorter code can only be better, right?

Quiz 14.1

With the variable-length binary code above, what is the string "001" an encoding of?

a) AB

b) CD

c) AAD

d) Not enough information to answer

(See Section 14.1.6 for the solution and discussion.)

The point of Quiz 14.1 is that, with variable-length codes and no further precautions, it can be unclear where one symbol starts and the next one begins. This problem does not arise with fixed-length codes. If every symbol is encoded using 6 bits, the second symbol always starts with the 7th bit, the third symbol with the 13th bit, and so on. With variable-length codes, we must impose a constraint to prevent ambiguity.

14.1.3   Prefix-Free Codes

We can eliminate all ambiguity by insisting that a code be *prefix-free*. This means that, for each pair of distinct symbols $a, b \in \Sigma$, the encoding of a is not a prefix of that of b, and vice versa. Every fixed-length code is automatically prefix-free. The variable-length code in the preceding section is not: The encoding of "A" is a prefix of that of "B," and similarly with "D" and "C."

With a prefix-free code, encodings are unambiguous and can be decoded in the obvious way. If the first 5 bits of a sequence match the encoding of a symbol a, then a was definitely the first symbol encoded—because the code is prefix-free, there's no way these 5 bits could correspond to (a prefix of) the encoding of any other symbol. If the next 7 bits match the encoding of b, then b was the second symbol encoded, and so on.

Here's an example of a prefix-free code for the alphabet $\Sigma = \{A, B, C, D\}$ that is not fixed-length:

Symbol	Encoding
A	0
B	10
C	110
D	111

Because "0" is used to encode A, the encodings of the other three symbols must start with a "1." Because B is encoded as "10," the encodings of C and D begin with "11."

14.1.4   The Benefits of Prefix-Free Codes

Variable-length prefix-free codes can be more efficient than fixed-length codes when the symbols have very different frequencies. For example, suppose we have the following statistics about symbol frequencies in our application (perhaps from past experience or from preprocessing the file to be encoded):

Symbol	Frequency
A	60%
B	25%
C	10%
D	5%

Let's compare the performance of our fixed-length and variable-length prefix-free codes:

Symbol	Fixed-length code	Variable-length prefix-free code
A	00	0
B	01	10
C	10	110
D	11	111

By "performance," we mean the average number of bits used to encode a symbol, with symbols weighted according to their frequencies. The fixed-length code always uses 2 bits, so this is also its average per-symbol length. What about the variable-length code? We might hope that it's better, given that it uses only 1 bit most of the time (60%) and resorts to 3 bits only in rare cases (15%).

Quiz 14.2

What is the average number of bits per symbol used by the variable-length code above?

   a) 1.5

   b) 1.55

   c) 2

   d) 2.5

(See Section 14.1.6 for the solution and discussion.)

14.1.5   Problem Definition

The preceding example shows that the best binary code for the job depends on the symbol frequencies. This means we have a super-cool algorithmic problem on our hands, which is the subject of the rest of this chapter.

Problem: Optimal Prefix-Free Codes

Input: A nonnegative frequency p_a for each symbol a of an alphabet Σ of size $n \geq 2$.

Output: The prefix-free binary code with minimum-possible average encoding length:

$$\sum_{a\in\Sigma} p_a \cdot (\text{number of bits used to encode } a).$$

How would you know in advance how frequent different symbols are? In some applications, there's plenty of data or domain knowledge. For example, any genomicist can tell you the typical frequency of each nucleobase (As, Cs, Gs, and Ts) in human DNA. In the case of encoding an MP3 file, the encoder computes symbol frequencies explicitly when preparing an initial digital version of the file (perhaps following an analog-to-digital conversion), and then uses an optimal prefix-free code to compress the file further.

The problem of computing an optimal prefix-free code looks intimidating at first encounter. The number of possible codes grows exponentially with n, so even for modest values of n there is no hope of exhaustively searching through all of them.[2] But surprisingly, the problem can be solved efficiently using a slick greedy algorithm.

14.1.6   Solutions to Quizzes 14.1–14.2

Solution to Quiz 14.1

Correct answer: (d). The proposed variable-length code creates ambiguity, and more than one sequence of symbols would lead to the encoding "001." One possibility is AB (encoded as "0" and "01," respectively), and another is AAD (encoded as "0," "0," and "1"). Given only the encoding, there's no way of knowing which meaning was intended.

---

[2]For example, there are $n!$ different prefix-free codes that encode one symbol using one bit ("0"), another using two bits ("10"), another using three bits ("110"), and so on.

Solution to Quiz 14.2

Correct answer: (b). Expanding out the weighted average, we have

$$\text{average \# of bits per symbol} = \underbrace{1 \cdot .6}_{\text{"}A\text{"}} + \underbrace{2 \cdot .25}_{\text{"}B\text{"}} + \underbrace{3 \cdot (.1 + .05)}_{\text{"}C\text{" and "}D\text{"}} = 1.55.$$

For this set of symbol frequencies, the variable-length code uses 22.5% fewer bits than the fixed-length code (on average)—a significant savings.

14.2 Codes as Trees

The "prefix-free" constraint in the optimal prefix-free code problem sounds a little scary. When putting together a code, how can we ensure that it's prefix-free? Crucial to reasoning about the problem is a method of associating codes with labeled binary trees.[3]

14.2.1 Three Examples

The connection between codes and trees is easiest to explain through examples. Our fixed-length code

Symbol	Encoding
A	00
B	01
C	10
D	11

can be represented via a complete binary tree with four leaves:

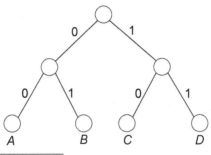

---

[3]Every node of a binary tree can have a left child, a right child, both, or neither. A node with no children is called a *leaf*. A non-leaf is also called an *internal node*. Both nodes and edges can be labeled. For some reason, computer scientists seem to think that trees grow downward, and they draw their trees accordingly.

Every edge connecting a node to its left or right child is labeled with a "0" or "1," respectively. The leaves of the tree are labeled with the four symbols of the alphabet. Every path from the root to a labeled node traverses two edges. We can interpret the labels of these two edges as an encoding of the leaf's symbol. For example, because the path from the root to the node labeled "B" traverses a left child edge ("0") followed by a right child edge ("1"), we can interpret the path as encoding the symbol B by 01. This matches B's encoding in our fixed-length code. The same is true for the other three symbols, as you should check.

Next, recall our first (non-prefix-free) variable-length code:

Symbol	Encoding
A	0
B	01
C	10
D	1

This code can be represented using a different labeled binary tree:

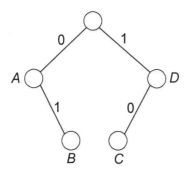

Once again there are four nodes labeled with the symbols of the alphabet—the two leaves and their parents. This tree defines an encoding for each symbol via the sequence of edge labels on the path from the root to the node labeled with that symbol. For example, going from the root to the node labeled "A" requires traversing only one left child edge, corresponding to the encoding "0." The encodings defined by this tree match those in the table above, as you should verify.

Finally, we can represent our prefix-free variable-length code

Symbol	Encoding
A	0
B	10
C	110
D	111

with the tree

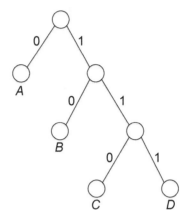

More generally, *every* binary code can be represented as a binary tree with left and right child edges labeled with "0" and "1," respectively, and with each symbol of the alphabet used as the label for exactly one node.[4] Conversely, every such tree defines a binary code, with the edge labels on the paths from the root to the labeled nodes providing the symbol encodings. The number of edges in a path equals the number of bits used to encode the corresponding symbol, so we have the following proposition.

Proposition 14.1 (Encoding Length and Tree Depth) *For every binary code, the encoding length in bits of a symbol $a \in \Sigma$ equals the depth of the node with label a in the corresponding tree.*

For example, in the prefix-free code above, the level-1 leaf corresponds to the symbol with a 1-bit encoding (A), the level-2 leaf to the symbol with a 2-bit encoding (B), and the level-3 leaves to the two symbols with 3-bit encodings (C and D).

---

[4]Suppose the largest number of bits used to encode a symbol is ℓ. Form a complete binary tree of depth ℓ. The encoding of each symbol a defines a path through the tree starting from the root, and the final node of this path should be labeled with a. Finally, repeatedly prune unlabeled leaves until none remain.

14.2.2   Which Trees Represent Prefix-Free Codes?

We've seen that binary trees can represent all binary codes, prefix-free or not. There's a dead giveaway when the code corresponding to a tree is not prefix-free.

For a clue, look at our three examples. The first and third trees, corresponding to the two prefix-free codes, look quite different from one another. But both share one property: Only the leaves are labeled with alphabet symbols. By contrast, two non-leaves are labeled in the second tree.

In general, the encoding of a symbol a is a prefix of that of another symbol b if and only if the node labeled a is an ancestor of the node labeled b. A labeled internal node is an ancestor of the (labeled) leaves in its subtree and leads to a violation of the prefix-free constraint.[5] Conversely, because no leaf can be the ancestor of another, a tree with labels only at the leaves defines a prefix-free code. Decoding a sequence of bits reduces to following your nose: Traverse the tree from top to bottom, taking a left or right turn whenever the next input bit is a 0 or 1, respectively. When a leaf is reached, its label indicates the next symbol in the sequence and the process restarts from the root with the remaining input bits. For example, with our third code, decoding the input "010111" results in three root-leaf traversals, terminating in A, then B, and finally D (Figure 14.1).

14.2.3   Problem Definition (Rephrased)

We can now restate the optimal prefix-free code problem in a particularly crisp form. By a Σ-*tree*, we mean a binary tree with leaves labeled in one-to-one correspondence with the symbols of Σ. As we've seen, prefix-free binary codes for an alphabet Σ correspond to Σ-trees.

For a Σ-tree T and symbol frequencies $\mathbf{p} = \{p_a\}_{a\in\Sigma}$, we denote by $L(T, \mathbf{p})$ the average depth of a leaf in T, with the contribution of each leaf weighted according to the frequency of its label:

$$L(T, \mathbf{p}) = \sum_{a\in\Sigma} p_a \cdot (\text{depth of the leaf labeled } a \text{ in } T). \qquad (14.1)$$

Proposition 14.1 implies that $L(T, \mathbf{p})$ is exactly the average encoding length of the code that corresponds to T, which is what we want to

---

[5]We can assume that every leaf of the tree has a label, as removing unlabeled leaves does not change the code defined by the tree.

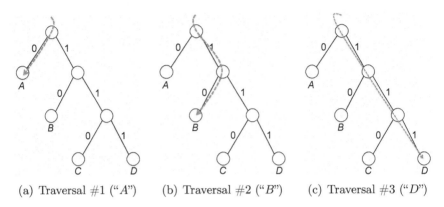

(a) Traversal #1 ("A")   (b) Traversal #2 ("B")   (c) Traversal #3 ("D")

Figure 14.1: Decoding the string "010111" to "ABD" by repeated root-leaf traversals.

minimize. We can therefore rephrase the optimal prefix-free code problem as a problem purely about binary trees.

Problem: Optimal Prefix-Free Codes (Rephrased)

Input: A nonnegative frequency p_a for each symbol a of an alphabet Σ of size $n \geq 2$.

Output: A Σ-tree with minimum-possible average leaf depth (14.1).

14.3 Huffman's Greedy Algorithm

14.3.1 Building Trees Through Successive Mergers

Huffman's big idea back in 1951 was to tackle the optimal prefix-free code problem using a bottom-up approach.[6] "Bottom-up" means starting with n nodes (where n is the size of the alphabet Σ), each labeled with a different symbol of Σ, and building up a tree through successive mergers. For example, if $\Sigma = \{A, B, C, D\}$, we start with what will be the leaves of the tree:

---

[6]This was for David A. Huffman's term paper in a class, believe it or not, and it superseded the (suboptimal) divide-and-conquer-esque top-down algorithm previously invented by Huffman's graduate advisor, Robert M. Fano.

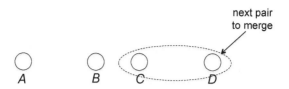

Our first merger might be of the nodes labeled "C" and "D," imple-mented by introducing one new unlabeled internal node with left and right children corresponding to C and D, respectively:

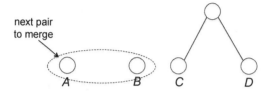

In effect, this merger commits to a tree in which the leaves labeled "C" and "D" are siblings (i.e., have a common parent).

Next we might do the same thing with A and B, committing further to a tree in which the leaves labeled "A" and "B" are siblings:

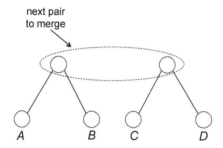

At this point, only two groups are left to merge. Merging them produces a full-blown binary tree:

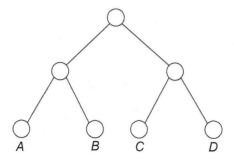

This binary tree is the same one used to represent the fixed-length code in Section 14.2.1.

Alternatively, in the second iteration we could merge the node labeled "*B*" with the tree containing "*C*" and "*D*":

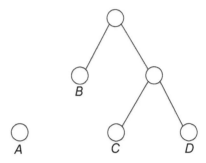

The final merge is again forced on us and produces the binary tree used to represent the variable-length prefix-free code in Section 14.2.1:

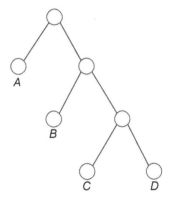

In general, Huffman's greedy algorithm maintains a *forest*, which is a collection of one or more binary trees. The leaves of the trees are in one-to-one correspondence with the symbols of Σ. Each iteration of the algorithm chooses two of the trees in the current forest and merges them by making their roots the left and right children of a new unlabeled internal node. The algorithm halts when only one tree remains.

Quiz 14.3

How many mergers will Huffman's greedy algorithm perform before halting? (Let $n = |\Sigma|$ denote the number of symbols.[7])

   a) $n - 1$

   b) n

   c) $\frac{(n+1)n}{2}$

   d) Not enough information to answer

(See Section 14.3.7 for the solution and discussion.)

14.3.2   Huffman's Greedy Criterion

For a given set of symbol frequencies $\{p_a\}_{a\in\Sigma}$, which pair of trees should we merge in each iteration? Each merger increments the depths of all the leaves in the two participating trees and, hence, the encoding lengths of the corresponding symbols. For example, in the penultimate merge above, the depth of the nodes labeled "C" and "D" increases from 1 to 2, and the depth of the node labeled "B" increases from 0 to 1. Every merger thus increases the objective function that we want to minimize: the average leaf depth (14.1). Every iteration of Huffman's greedy algorithm myopically performs the merge that least increases this objective function.

Huffman's Greedy Criterion

Merge the pair of trees that causes the minimum-possible increase in the average leaf depth.

By how much does a merger increase the average leaf depth? For every symbol a in one of the two participating trees, the depth of the corresponding leaf goes up by 1 and so the contribution of the corresponding term in the sum (14.1) goes up by p_a. Thus, merging two trees T_1 and T_2 increases the average leaf depth by the sum of the frequencies of the participating symbols:

$$\sum_{a\in T_1} p_a + \sum_{a\in T_2} p_a, \qquad (14.2)$$

---

[7]For a finite set S, $|S|$ denotes the number of elements in S.

where the summations are over all the alphabet symbols for which the corresponding leaf belongs to T_1 or T_2, respectively. Huffman's greedy criterion then dictates that we merge the pair of trees for which the sum (14.2) is as small as possible.

14.3.3 Pseudocode

As advertised, Huffman's algorithm builds a Σ-tree bottom-up, and in every iteration it merges the two trees that have the smallest sums of corresponding symbol frequencies.

Huffman

Input: a nonnegative frequency p_a for each symbol a of an alphabet Σ.
Output: the Σ-tree with minimum average leaf depth, representing the prefix-free binary code with minimum average encoding length.

```
// Initialization
for each a ∈ Σ do
    T_a := tree containing one node, labeled "a"
    P(T_a) := p_a
F := {T_a}_{a∈Σ}   // invariant: ∀T ∈ F, P(T) = Σ_{a∈T} p_a
// Main loop
while F contains at least two trees do
    T_1 := argmin_{T∈F} P(T)        // min frequency sum
    T_2 := argmin_{T∈F,T≠T_1} P(T)  // second-smallest
    remove T_1 and T_2 from F
    // roots of T_1, T_2 become left, right
        children of a new internal node
    T_3 := merger of T_1 and T_2
    P(T_3) := P(T_1) + P(T_2) // maintains invariant
    add T_3 to F
return the unique tree in F
```

On Pseudocode

This book series explains algorithms using a mixture of high-level pseudocode and English (as above). I'm assuming that you have the skills to translate such high-level descriptions into working code in your favorite programming language. Several other books and resources on the Web offer concrete implementations of various algorithms in specific programming languages.

The first benefit of emphasizing high-level descriptions over language-specific implementations is flexibility. While I assume familiarity with *some* programming language, I don't care which one. Second, this approach promotes the understanding of algorithms at a deep and conceptual level, unencumbered by low-level details. Seasoned programmers and computer scientists generally think and communicate about algorithms at a similarly high level.

Still, there is no substitute for the detailed understanding of an algorithm that comes from providing your own working implementation of it. I strongly encourage you to implement as many of the algorithms in this book as you have time for. (It's also a great excuse to pick up a new programming language!) For guidance, see the end-of-chapter Programming Problems and supporting test cases.

14.3.4   Example

For example, let's return to our four-symbol alphabet with the following frequencies:

Symbol	Frequency
A	.60
B	.25
C	.10
D	.05

Initially, the `Huffman` algorithm creates a forest of four trees, T_A, T_B, T_C, T_D, each containing one node labeled with a different alphabet symbol. The first iteration of the algorithm merges the nodes that correspond to the two symbols with the smallest frequencies—in this case, "C" and "D." After this iteration, the algorithm's forest contains only three trees, with the following sums of symbol frequencies:

Symbol	Sum of Symbol Frequencies
tree containing A	.60
tree containing B	.25
tree containing C and D	$.05 + .10 = .15$

The second two trees have the smallest sums of symbol frequencies, so these are the trees merged in the second iteration. In the third iteration, the forest $\mathcal{F}$ contains only two trees; they are merged to produce the final output, which is exactly the tree used to represent the variable-length prefix-free code in Section 14.2.1:

14.3.5   A Larger Example

To ensure that Huffman's greedy algorithm is crystal clear, let's see how the final tree takes shape in a larger example:

Symbol	Frequency
A	3
B	2
C	6
D	8
E	2
F	6

If it bothers you that the symbol frequencies don't add up to 1, feel free to divide each of them by 27; it doesn't change the problem.

As usual, the first step merges the two symbols with the smallest frequencies, namely "B" and "E":

The five trees left in the forest are

Symbol	Sum of Symbol Frequencies
tree containing A	3
tree containing C	6
tree containing D	8
tree containing F	6
tree containing B and E	$2+2=4$

and the algorithm next merges the first and last of these:

The four remaining trees are

Symbol	Sum of Symbol Frequencies
tree containing C	6
tree containing D	8
tree containing F	6
tree containing A, B and E	$4+3=7$

Next the algorithm merges the nodes labeled "C" and "F":

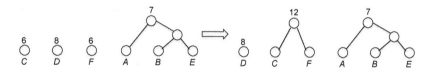

and three trees remain:

Symbol	Sum of Symbol Frequencies
tree containing D	8
tree containing C and F	$6+6=12$
tree containing A, B and E	7

The penultimate merge is of the first and third trees:

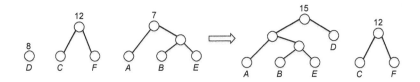

and the final merge produces the output of the algorithm:

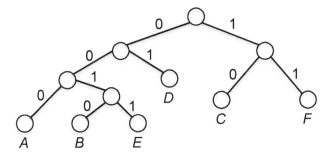

This tree corresponds to the following prefix-free code:

Symbol	Encoding
A	000
B	0010
C	10
D	01
E	0011
F	11

14.3.6   Running Time

A straightforward implementation of the Huffman algorithm runs in $O(n^2)$ time, where n is the number of symbols. As noted in Quiz 14.3, each merge decreases the number of trees in $\mathcal{F}$ by 1, resulting in $n-1$ iterations of the main loop. Each iteration is responsible for identifying the two current trees with the smallest sums of symbol frequencies; this can be done by exhaustive search over the $O(n)$ trees of $\mathcal{F}$. The rest of the work—initialization, updating $\mathcal{F}$, rewiring pointers when merging two trees—contributes only $O(n)$ operations to the overall running time bound, for a total of $O(n^2)$.

Readers familiar with the heap data structure (covered in Chapter 10 of *Part 2* and reviewed in Section 15.3) should spot an opportunity to do better. The raison d'être of the heap data structure is to speed up repeated minimum computations so that each computation takes logarithmic rather than linear time. The work performed in each iteration of the main loop in the `Huffman` algorithm is dominated by two minimum computations, so a light bulb should go off in your head: This algorithm calls out for a heap! Using a heap to speed up these minimum computations decreases the running time from $O(n^2)$ to $O(n \log n)$, which qualifies as a blazingly fast implementation.[8]

We can do even better. The `Huffman` algorithm can be implemented by sorting the symbols in order of increasing frequency and then performing a linear amount of additional processing. This implementation eschews heaps in favor of an even simpler data structure: a queue (actually, two queues). See Problem 14.5 for more details. The n symbols can be sorted by frequency in $O(n \log n)$ time (see footnote 3 of Chapter 13), so the running time of this implementation is $O(n \log n)$. Moreover, in the special cases in which sorting is possible in linear time, this implementation of the `Huffman` algorithm also runs in linear time.[9]

14.3.7   Solution to Quiz 14.3

Correct answer: (a). The initial forest has n trees, where n is the number of alphabet symbols. Each merge replaces a pair of trees with a single tree and, hence, decreases the number of trees by 1. The algorithm halts once one tree remains, which is after $n - 1$ mergers.

*14.4   Proof of Correctness

The `Huffman` algorithm correctly solves the optimal prefix-free code problem.[10]

---

[8]The objects in the heap correspond to the trees of $\mathcal{F}$. The key associated with an object is the sum of the frequencies of the symbols that correspond to the tree's leaves. In each iteration, the trees T_1 and T_2 can be removed from the heap using two successive EXTRACTMIN operations, and the merged tree T_3 added with one INSERT operation (with T_3's key set to the sum of the keys of T_1 and T_2).

[9]The best-possible running time of a "general-purpose" sorting algorithm, which makes no assumptions about the data to be sorted, is $O(n \log n)$. With additional assumptions, however, specialized sorting algorithms can do better. For example, if every element to be sorted is an integer with magnitude at most n^{10} (say), the RadixSort algorithm can be used to sort them in $O(n)$ time. See Section 5.6 of *Part 1* for a full discussion.

[10]Starred sections like this one are the more difficult sections; they can be skipped on a first reading.

Theorem 14.2 (Correctness of Huffman) *For every alphabet* Σ *and nonnegative symbol frequencies* $\{p_a\}_{a \in \Sigma}$, *the* **Huffman** *algorithm outputs a prefix-free code with the minimum-possible average encoding length.*

Equivalently, the algorithm outputs a Σ-tree with the minimum-possible average leaf depth (14.1).

14.4.1   High-Level Plan

The proof of Theorem 14.2 blends two common strategies for correctness proofs of greedy algorithms, both mentioned in Section 13.4: induction and exchange arguments.

We'll proceed by induction on the size of the alphabet, with two ideas required to implement the inductive step. Fix from now on an input, with alphabet Σ and symbol frequencies **p**, and let a and b denote the symbols with the smallest and second-smallest frequencies, respectively. Consider the first iteration of the Huffman algorithm, in which it merges the leaves that correspond to a and b. The algorithm has then effectively committed to a Σ-tree in which (the leaves corresponding to) a and b are siblings. The first main idea is to prove that, among all such trees, the Huffman algorithm outputs the best one.

Main Idea #1

Prove that the output of the Huffman algorithm minimizes the average leaf depth over all Σ-trees in which a and b are siblings.

This step boils down to showing that the problem of computing the best Σ-tree in which a and b are siblings is equivalent to that of computing the best Σ'-tree, where Σ' is the same as Σ except with a and b fused into a single symbol. Because Σ' is a smaller alphabet than Σ, we can complete the proof using induction.

This first idea is not enough. If every Σ-tree with a and b as siblings is suboptimal, it does us no good to optimize over them. The second main idea resolves this worry and proves that it's always safe to commit to a tree in which the two lowest-frequency symbols correspond to sibling leaves.

> ### Main Idea #2
>
> Prove that there is an optimal Σ-tree in which a and b are siblings.

The idea here is to show that every Σ-tree can be massaged into an equally good or better Σ-tree in which a and b are siblings, by exchanging the labels a and b with the labels x and y of two leaves in the tree's deepest level. Intuitively, it's a net win to demote the smaller-frequency symbols a and b to the deepest level of the tree while promoting the higher-frequency symbols x and y closer to the root.

If both main ideas can be implemented, the inductive step and Theorem 14.2 follow easily. The first idea implies that the Huffman algorithm solves the problem optimally over a restricted family of Σ-trees, those in which a and b are siblings. The second guarantees that an optimal tree of this restricted type is, in fact, optimal for the original problem.

14.4.2   The Details

Induction Review

For the formal proof, we turn to our old friend (or is it nemesis?), induction.[11] Recall that proofs by induction follow a fairly rigid template, with the goal of establishing that an assertion $P(k)$ holds for arbitrarily large positive integers k. In the proof of Theorem 14.2, we take $P(k)$ as the statement:

> "the Huffman algorithm correctly solves the optimal prefix-free code problem whenever the alphabet size is at most k."

Analogous to a recursive algorithm, a proof by induction has two parts: a *base case* and an *inductive step*. For us, the natural base case is the statement $P(2)$. (The optimal prefix-free code problem is uninteresting with a one-symbol alphabet.) In the inductive step, we assume that $k > 2$. We also assume that $P(2), P(3), \ldots, P(k-1)$ are all true—this is called the *inductive hypothesis*—and use this

---

[11] For an induction refresher, see Appendix A of *Part 1* or the book *Mathematics for Computer Science* mentioned in the Preface.

assumption to prove that $P(k)$ is consequently true as well. If we prove both the base case and the inductive step, then $P(k)$ is indeed true for every positive integer $k \geq 2$: $P(2)$ is true by the base case and, like falling dominoes, applying the inductive step over and over again shows that $P(k)$ is true for arbitrarily large values of k.

The Huffman algorithm is optimal for two-symbol alphabets: The algorithm uses 1 bit to encode each symbol (0 for one symbol and 1 for the other), which is the minimum possible. This proves the base case.

For the inductive step, assume that $k > 2$ and fix an alphabet Σ of size k and nonnegative symbol frequencies $\mathbf{p} = \{p_x\}_{x \in \Sigma}$. For the rest of the proof, we denote by a and b the two symbols of Σ with the smallest and second-smallest frequencies, respectively. (Break ties arbitrarily.)

The First Main Idea, Restated

To implement the first and more difficult main idea from Section 14.4.1, define

$$\mathcal{T}_{ab} = \left\{ \begin{array}{l} \Sigma\text{-trees in which } a \text{ and } b \text{ are the left and right} \\ \text{children of a common parent, respectively} \end{array} \right\}.$$

The Huffman algorithm outputs a tree of $\mathcal{T}_{ab}$, and we want to prove that it is the best such tree:

(*)   among all trees in $\mathcal{T}_{ab}$, the Huffman algorithm outputs one with the minimum-possible average leaf depth.

As a reminder, the average leaf depth of a Σ-tree T with respect to the symbol frequencies $\mathbf{p}$ is

$$L(T, \mathbf{p}) = \sum_{x \in \Sigma} p_x \cdot (\text{depth of the leaf labeled } x \text{ in } T).$$

This quantity is the same as the average encoding length of the corresponding prefix-free code.

Applying the Inductive Hypothesis to a Residual Problem

The inductive hypothesis applies only to alphabets with less than k symbols. So derive Σ' from Σ by fusing the symbols a and b—the symbols with the smallest and second-smallest frequencies—into a single "meta-symbol" ab. There is a one-to-one correspondence between Σ'-trees and the restricted set $\mathcal{T}_{ab}$ of Σ-trees (Figure 14.2). Every Σ'-tree T' can be transformed into a Σ-tree $T \in \mathcal{T}_{ab}$ by replacing the leaf labeled "ab" with an unlabeled node that has children labeled "a" and "b." We denote this mapping $T' \mapsto T$ by $\beta(T')$. Conversely, every tree $T \in \mathcal{T}_{ab}$ can be turned into a Σ'-tree T' by sucking the leaves labeled a and b into their (common) parent and labeling the resulting "meta-node" with "ab." We denote this inverse mapping $T \mapsto T'$ by $\alpha(T)$.

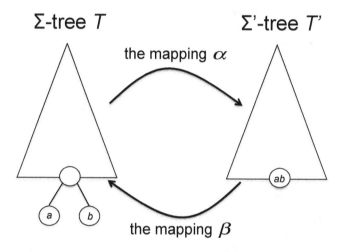

Figure 14.2: There is a one-to-one correspondence between Σ'-trees and the Σ-trees in which a and b are the left and right children of a common parent.

The frequencies $\mathbf{p}' = \{p'_x\}_{x \in \Sigma'}$ we assign to the symbols of Σ' match those of Σ, except with the frequency p'_{ab} of the new symbol ab defined as the sum $p_a + p_b$ of the frequencies of the two symbols it represents.

The first iteration of the `Huffman` algorithm merges the leaves labeled "a" and "b" and thereafter treats them as an indivisible unit with total frequency $p_a + p_b$. This means the final output of the algorithm is the same as if it had been restarted from scratch with the input Σ' and $\mathbf{p}'$, with the resulting Σ'-tree translated by the mapping β back to a Σ-tree of $\mathcal{T}_{ab}$.

Proposition 14.3 (Preservation of Behavior of Huffman) *The output of the Huffman algorithm with input Σ and $\mathbf{p}$ is $\beta(T')$, where T' is the output of the Huffman algorithm with input Σ' and $\mathbf{p}'$.*

Additional Properties of the Correspondence

The correspondence between Σ'-trees and the Σ-trees in $\mathcal{T}_{ab}$ given by the mappings α and β (Figure 14.2) also preserves the average leaf depth, up to a constant that is independent of the choice of tree.

Proposition 14.4 (Preservation of Average Leaf Depth) *For every Σ-tree T of $\mathcal{T}_{ab}$ with symbol frequencies $\mathbf{p}$ and corresponding Σ'-tree $T' = \alpha(T)$ and symbol frequencies $\mathbf{p}'$,*

$$L(T, \mathbf{p}) = L(T', \mathbf{p}') + \underbrace{p_a + p_b}_{\textit{independent of } T} \quad .$$

Proof: Leaves of T not labeled a or b occupy the same position in T'. Their symbols have the same frequencies in $\mathbf{p}$ and $\mathbf{p}'$, so these leaves contribute the same amount to the average leaf depth of both trees. The total frequency of a and b in $\mathbf{p}$ is the same as that of ab in $\mathbf{p}'$, but the depth of the corresponding leaves is one larger. Thus, the contribution of a and b to the average leaf depth of T is $p_a + p_b$ larger than the contribution of ab to the average leaf depth of T'. $\mathcal{QED}$

Because the correspondence between Σ'-trees and the Σ-trees in $\mathcal{T}_{ab}$ preserves the average leaf depth (up to the tree-independent constant $p_a + p_b$), it associates the optimal Σ'-tree with the optimal Σ-tree in $\mathcal{T}_{ab}$:

$$\text{best } \Sigma\text{-tree in } \mathcal{T}_{ab} \underset{\beta}{\overset{\alpha}{\rightleftharpoons}} \text{ best } \Sigma'\text{-tree}$$

$$\text{second-best } \Sigma\text{-tree in } \mathcal{T}_{ab} \underset{\beta}{\overset{\alpha}{\rightleftharpoons}} \text{ second-best } \Sigma'\text{-tree}$$

$$\vdots$$

$$\text{worst } \Sigma\text{-tree in } \mathcal{T}_{ab} \underset{\beta}{\overset{\alpha}{\rightleftharpoons}} \text{ worst } \Sigma'\text{-tree}.$$

Corollary 14.5 (Preservation of Optimal Solutions)
A Σ'-tree T^* minimizes $L(T', \mathbf{p}')$ over all Σ'-trees T' if and only if the corresponding Σ-tree $\beta(T^*)$ minimizes $L(T, \mathbf{p})$ over all Σ-trees T in $\mathcal{T}_{ab}$.

Implementing the First Main Idea

We now have all our ducks in a row for proving the statement (*), that among all trees of $\mathcal{T}_{ab}$, the Huffman algorithm outputs one with the minimum-possible average leaf depth:

1. By Proposition 14.3, the output of the Huffman algorithm with input Σ and $\mathbf{p}$ is $\beta(T')$, where T' is the output of the Huffman algorithm with input Σ' and $\mathbf{p}'$.

2. Because $|\Sigma'| < k$, the inductive hypothesis implies that the output T' of the Huffman algorithm with input Σ' and $\mathbf{p}'$ is optimal.

3. By Corollary 14.5, the Σ-tree $\beta(T')$ is optimal for the original problem with input Σ and $\mathbf{p}$.

Implementing the Second Main Idea

The second part of the inductive step is easier and based on an exchange argument. Here, we want to prove that the Huffman algorithm did not make a mistake by committing to a tree in which the two smallest-frequency symbols are siblings:

(†) There is a tree of $\mathcal{T}_{ab}$ that minimizes the average leaf depth $L(T, \mathbf{p})$ over all Σ-trees T.

To prove (†), consider an arbitrary Σ-tree T. We can complete the proof by exhibiting a tree $T^* \in \mathcal{T}_{ab}$ in which a and b are siblings such that $L(T^*, \mathbf{p}) \leq L(T, \mathbf{p})$. Without loss of generality, each node of T either is a leaf or has two children.[12] Thus, there are two leaves with a common parent that inhabit the deepest level of T, say with left child x and right child y.[13] Obtain the Σ-tree $T^* \in \mathcal{T}_{ab}$ by exchanging

---

[12] An internal node with only one child can be spliced out to give another Σ-tree with smaller average leaf depth.

[13] For simplicity, you can think of x and y as distinct from a and b, but the proof works fine even when $\{x, y\}$ and $\{a, b\}$ overlap (as you should check).

the labels of the leaves labeled "a" and "x," and the labels of the leaves labeled "b" and "y":

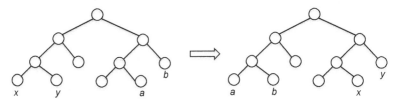

How does the average leaf depth change? Expanding the definition (14.1) and canceling the terms that correspond to leaves other than a, b, x, y, we have

$$L(T) - L(T^*) = \sum_{z \in \{a,b,x,y\}} p_z \cdot (\text{depth of } z \text{ in } T - \text{depth of } z \text{ in } T^*).$$

Depths in T^* can be rewritten in terms of depths in T. For example, the depth of a in T^* is the same as the depth of x in T, the depth of y in T^* is the same as the depth of b in T, and so on. We can therefore sneakily rearrange terms to obtain

$$L(T) - L(T^*) = \underbrace{(p_x - p_a)}_{\geq 0} \cdot \underbrace{(\text{depth of } x \text{ in } T - \text{depth of } a \text{ in } T)}_{\geq 0}$$
$$+ \underbrace{(p_y - p_b)}_{\geq 0} \cdot \underbrace{(\text{depth of } y \text{ in } T - \text{depth of } b \text{ in } T)}_{\geq 0}$$
$$\geq 0.$$

The rearrangement makes it obvious that the difference on the left-hand side is nonnegative: $p_x - p_a$ and $p_y - p_b$ are nonnegative because a and b were chosen as the symbols with the smallest frequencies, and the other two terms on the right-hand side are nonnegative because x and y were chosen from the deepest level of T. We conclude that the average leaf depth of $T^* \in \mathcal{T}_{ab}$ is at most that of T. Because every Σ-tree is equaled or bettered by a tree of $\mathcal{T}_{ab}$, $\mathcal{T}_{ab}$ contains a tree that is optimal among all Σ-trees. This wraps up the proof of (†).

To recap, the statement (*) implies that, with the input Σ and $\mathbf{p}$, the `Huffman` algorithm outputs the best-possible tree from the restricted set $\mathcal{T}_{ab}$. By (†), this tree must be optimal for the original problem. This completes the proof of the inductive step and of Theorem 14.2. $\mathcal{QED}$

The Upshot

★ Prefix-free variable-length binary codes can have smaller average encoding lengths than fixed-length codes when different alphabet symbols have different frequencies.

★ Prefix-free codes can be visualized as binary trees in which the leaves are in one-to-one correspondence with the alphabet symbols. Encodings correspond to root-leaf paths, with left and right child edges interpreted as 0s and 1s, respectively, while the average encoding length corresponds to the average leaf depth.

★ Huffman's greedy algorithm maintains a forest, with leaves in correspondence to alphabet symbols, and in each iteration greedily merges the pair of trees that causes the minimum-possible increase in the average leaf depth.

★ Huffman's algorithm is guaranteed to compute a prefix-free code with the minimum-possible average encoding length.

★ Huffman's algorithm can be implemented in $O(n \log n)$ time, where n is the number of symbols.

★ The proof of correctness uses an exchange argument to show the existence of an optimal solution in which the two smallest-frequency symbols are siblings, and induction to show that the algorithm computes such a solution.

Test Your Understanding

Problem 14.1 *(S)* Consider the following symbol frequencies for a five-symbol alphabet:

Symbol	Frequency
A	.32
B	.25
C	.2
D	.18
E	.05

What is the average encoding length of an optimal prefix-free code?

a) 2.23

b) 2.4

c) 3

d) 3.45

Problem 14.2 *(S)* Consider the following symbol frequencies for a five-symbol alphabet:

Symbol	Frequency
A	.16
B	.08
C	.35
D	.07
E	.34

What is the average encoding length of an optimal prefix-free code?

a) 2.11

b) 2.31

c) 2.49

d) 2.5

Problem 14.3 *(H)* What is the maximum number of bits that Huffman's greedy algorithm might use to encode a single symbol? (As usual, $n = |\Sigma|$ denotes the alphabet size.)

a) $\log_2 n$

b) $\ln n$

c) $n - 1$

d) n

Problem 14.4 *(H)* Which of the following statements about Huffman's greedy algorithm are true? Assume that the symbol frequencies sum to 1. (Choose all that apply.)

a) A letter with frequency at least 0.4 will never be encoded with two or more bits.

b) A letter with frequency at least 0.5 will never be encoded with two or more bits.

c) If all symbol frequencies are less than 0.33, all symbols will be encoded with at least two bits.

d) If all symbol frequencies are less than 0.5, all symbols will be encoded with at least two bits.

Challenge Problems

Problem 14.5 *(S)* Give an implementation of Huffman's greedy algorithm that uses a single invocation of a sorting subroutine, followed by a linear amount of additional work.

Programming Problems

Problem 14.6 Implement in your favorite programming language the `Huffman` algorithm from Section 14.3 for the optimal prefix-free code problem. How much faster is the heap-based implementation (outlined in footnote 8) than the straightforward quadratic-time implementation?[14] How much faster is the implementation in Problem 14.5 than the heap-based implementation? (See `www.algorithmsilluminated.org` for test cases and challenge data sets.)

---

[14]Don't forget to check if the heap data structure is built in to your favorite programming language, such as the `PriorityQueue` class in Java.

Chapter 15

Minimum Spanning Trees

This chapter applies the greedy algorithm design paradigm to a famous graph problem, the *minimum spanning tree (MST)* problem.
The MST problem is a uniquely great playground for the study of
greedy algorithms, in which almost any greedy algorithm that you
can think of turns out to be correct. After reviewing graphs and
defining the problem formally (Section 15.1), we'll discuss the two
best-known MST algorithms—Prim's algorithm (Section 15.2) and
Kruskal's algorithm (Section 15.5). Both algorithms admit blazingly
fast implementations, using the heap and union-find data structures,
respectively. Section 15.8 outlines an application of Kruskal's algorithm in machine learning, to single-link clustering.

15.1 Problem Definition

The minimum spanning tree problem is about connecting a bunch
of objects as cheaply as possible. The objects and connections could
represent something physical, like computer servers and communica-
tion links between them. Or maybe each object is a representation of
a document (say, as a vector of word frequencies), with connections
corresponding to pairs of "similar" documents. The problem arises naturally in several application domains, including computer networking
(try a Web search for "spanning tree protocol") and machine learning
(see Section 15.8).

15.1.1 Graphs

Objects and connections between them are most naturally modeled
with graphs. A *graph* $G = (V, E)$ has two ingredients: a set V of
vertices and a set E of *edges* (Figure 15.1). This chapter considers only
undirected graphs, in which each edge e is an unordered pair $\{v, w\}$

of vertices (written as $e = (v, w)$ or $e = (w, v)$), which are called the *endpoints* of the edge.[1] The numbers $|V|$ and $|E|$ of vertices and edges are usually denoted by n and m, respectively.

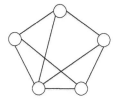

Figure 15.1: An undirected graph with five vertices and eight edges.

Graphs can be encoded in different ways for use in an algorithm. This chapter assumes that the input graph is represented using adjacency lists, with an array of vertices, an array of edges, pointers from each edge to its two endpoints, and pointers from each vertex to its incident edges.[2]

15.1.2   Spanning Trees

The input in the minimum spanning tree problem is an undirected graph $G = (V, E)$ in which each edge e has a real-valued cost c_e. (For example, c_e could indicate the cost of connecting two computer servers.) The goal is to compute a spanning tree of the graph with the minimum-possible sum of edge costs. By a *spanning tree* of G, we mean a subset $T \subseteq E$ of edges that satisfies two properties. First, T should not contain a cycle (this is the "tree" part).[3] Second, for every pair $v, w \in V$ of vertices, T should include a path between v and w (this is the "spanning" part).[4]

---

[1] There is an analog of the MST problem for directed graphs, which is known as both the *minimum-cost arborescence problem* and the *optimum branching problem*. There are also fast algorithms for this problem, but they lie a bit beyond the scope of this book series.

[2] For more details on graphs and their representations, see Chapter 7 of *Part 2*.

[3] A *cycle* in a graph $G = (V, E)$ is a path that loops back to where it began—an edge sequence $e_1 = (v_0, v_1), e_2 = (v_1, v_2), \ldots, e_k = (v_{k-1}, v_k)$ with $v_k = v_0$.

[4] For convenience, we typically allow a path $(v_0, v_1), (v_1, v_2), \ldots, (v_{k-1}, v_k)$ in a graph to include repeated vertices or, equivalently, to contain one or more cycles. Don't let this bother you: You can always convert such a path into a cycle-free path with the same endpoints v_0 and v_k by repeatedly splicing out subpaths between different visits to the same vertex (see Figure 15.2 below).

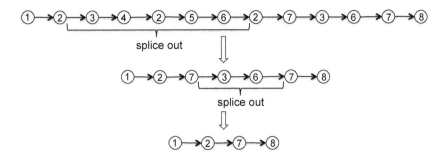

Figure 15.2: A path with repeated vertices can be converted into a path with no repeated vertices and the same endpoints.

Quiz 15.1

What is the minimum sum of edge costs of a spanning tree of the following graph? (Each edge is labeled with its cost.)

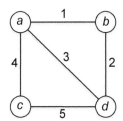

a) 6

b) 7

c) 8

d) 9

(See Section 15.1.3 for the solution and discussion.)

It makes sense only to talk about spanning trees of *connected* graphs $G = (V, E)$, in which it's possible to travel from any vertex $v \in V$ to any other vertex $w \in V$ using a path of edges in E.[5] (If there

---

[5]For example, the graph in Figure 15.1 is connected, while the graph in Figure 15.3 is not.

is no path in E between the vertices v and w, there certainly isn't one in any subset $T \subseteq E$ of edges, either.) For this reason, throughout this chapter we assume that the input graph is a connected graph.

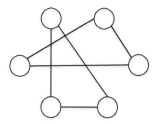

Figure 15.3: A graph that is not connected.

MST Assumption

The input graph $G = (V, E)$ is connected, with at least one path between each pair of vertices.

It's easy enough to compute the minimum spanning tree of a four-vertex graph like the one in Quiz 15.1; what about in general?

Problem: Minimum Spanning Tree (MST)

Input: A connected undirected graph $G = (V, E)$ and a real-valued cost c_e for each edge $e \in E$.

Output: A spanning tree $T \subseteq E$ of G with the minimum-possible sum $\sum_{e \in T} c_e$ of edge costs.[6]

We can assume that the input graph has at most one edge between each pair of vertices; all but the cheapest of a set of parallel edges can be thrown out without changing the problem.

---

[6]For graphs that are not connected, we could instead consider the minimum spanning *forest* problem, in which the goal is to find a maximal acyclic subgraph with the minimum-possible sum of edge costs. This problem can be solved by first computing the connected components of the input graph in linear time using breadth- or depth-first search (see Chapter 8 of *Part 2*), and then applying an algorithm for the MST problem to each component separately.

Like minimizing the sum of weighted completion times (Chapter 13) or the optimal prefix-free code problem (Chapter 14), the number of possible solutions can be exponential in the size of the problem.[7] Could there be an algorithm that magically homes in on the minimum-cost needle in the haystack of spanning trees?

15.1.3   Solution to Quiz 15.1

Correct answer: (b). The minimum spanning tree comprises the edges (a, b), (b, d), and (a, c):

The sum of the edges' costs is 7. The edges do not include a cycle, and they can be used to travel from any vertex to any other vertex.

Here are two spanning trees with an inferior total cost of 8:

 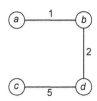

The three edges (a, b), (b, d), and (a, d) have a smaller total cost of 6:

but these edges do not form a spanning tree. In fact, they fail on both counts: They form a cycle and there is no way to use them to travel from c to any other vertex.

---

[7]For example, *Cayley's formula* is a famous result from combinatorics stating that the n-vertex complete graph (in which all the $\binom{n}{2}$ possible edges are present) has exactly n^{n-2} different spanning trees. This is bigger than the estimated number of atoms in the known universe when $n \geq 50$.

15.2   Prim's Algorithm

Our first algorithm for the minimum spanning tree problem is *Prim's algorithm*, which is named after Robert C. Prim, who discovered the algorithm in 1957. The algorithm closely resembles Dijkstra's shortest-path algorithm (covered in Chapter 9 of *Part 2*), so it shouldn't surprise you that Edsger W. Dijkstra independently arrived at the same algorithm shortly thereafter, in 1959. Only later was it realized that the algorithm had been discovered over 25 years earlier, by Vojtěch Jarník in 1930. For this reason, the algorithm is also called *Jarník's algorithm* and the *Prim-Jarník algorithm.*[8]

15.2.1   Example

Next we'll step through Prim's algorithm on a concrete example, the same one from Quiz 15.1:

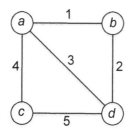

It might seem weird to go through an example of an algorithm before you've seen its code, but trust me: After you understand the example, the pseudocode will practically write itself.[9]

Prim's algorithm begins by choosing an arbitrary vertex—let's say vertex *b* in our example. (In the end, it won't matter which one we pick.) The plan is to construct a tree one edge at a time, starting from *b* and growing like a mold until the tree spans the entire vertex set. In each iteration, we'll greedily add the cheapest edge that extends the reach of the tree-so-far.

---

[8] History buffs should check out the paper "On the History of the Minimum Spanning Tree Problem," by Ronald L. Graham and Pavol Hell (*Annals of the History of Computing*, 1985).

[9] Readers of *Part 2* should recognize strong similarities to Dijkstra's shortest-path algorithm.

The algorithm's initial (empty) tree spans only the starting vertex b. There are two options for expanding its reach: the edge (a, b) and the edge (b, d).

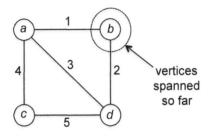

The former is cheaper, so the algorithm chooses it. The tree-so-far spans the vertices a and b.

In the second iteration, three edges would expand the tree's reach: (a, c), (a, d), and (b, d).

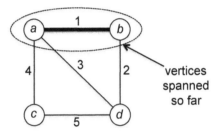

The cheapest of these is (b, d). After its addition, the tree-so-far spans a, b, and d. Both endpoints of the edge (a, d) have been sucked into the set of vertices spanned so far; adding this edge in the future would create a cycle, so the algorithm does not consider it further.

In the final iteration, there are two options for expanding the tree's reach to c, the edges (a, c) and (c, d):

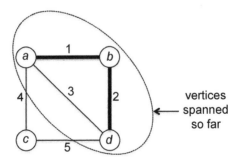

Prim's algorithm chooses the cheaper edge (a, c), resulting in the same minimum spanning tree identified in Quiz 15.1:

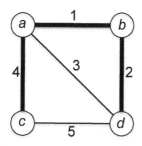

15.2.2   Pseudocode

In general, Prim's algorithm grows a spanning tree from a starting vertex one edge at a time, with each iteration extending the reach of the tree-so-far by one additional vertex. As a greedy algorithm, the algorithm always chooses the cheapest edge that does the job.

Prim

Input: connected undirected graph $G = (V, E)$ in adjacency-list representation and a cost c_e for each edge $e \in E$.

Output: the edges of a minimum spanning tree of G.

```
// Initialization
X := {s}    // s is an arbitrarily chosen vertex
T := ∅      // invariant: the edges in T span X
// Main loop
while there is an edge (v, w) with v ∈ X, w ∉ X do
    (v*, w*) := a minimum-cost such edge
    add vertex w* to X
    add edge (v*, w*) to T
return T
```

The sets T and X keep track of the edges chosen and the vertices spanned so far. The algorithm seeds X with an arbitrarily chosen starting vertex s; as we'll see, the algorithm is correct no matter

which vertex it chooses.[10] Each iteration is responsible for adding
one new edge to T. To avoid redundant edges and ensure that the
edge addition extends the reach of T, the algorithm considers only
the edges that "cross the frontier," with one endpoint in each of X
and $V - X$ (Figure 15.4). If there are many such edges, the algorithm
greedily chooses the cheapest one. After $n - 1$ iterations (where n is
the number of vertices), X contains all the vertices and the algorithm
halts. Under our assumption that the input graph G is connected,
there's no way for the algorithm to get stuck; if there were ever an
iteration with no edges of G crossing between X and $V - X$, we could
conclude that G is not connected (because it contains no path from
any vertex in X to any vertex in $V - X$).

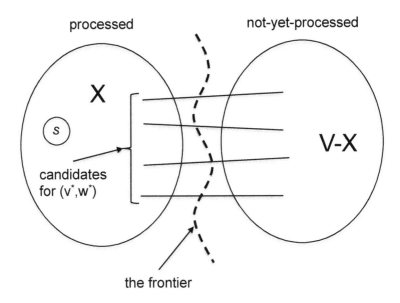

Figure 15.4: Every iteration of Prim's algorithm chooses one new edge
that crosses from X to $V - X$.

---

[10]The MST problem definition makes no reference to a starting vertex, so
it might seem weird to artificially introduce one here. One big benefit is that
a starting vertex allows us to closely mimic Dijkstra's shortest-path algorithm
(which is saddled with a starting vertex by the problem it solves, the single-source
shortest path problem). And it doesn't really change the problem: Connecting
every pair of vertices is the same thing as connecting some vertex s to every other
vertex. (To get a v-w path, paste together paths from v to s and from s to w.)

The algorithm `Prim` computes the minimum spanning tree in the four-vertex five-edge graph of Quiz 15.1, which means approximately... nothing. The fact that an algorithm works correctly on a specific example does *not* imply that it is correct in general![11] You should be initially skeptical of the `Prim` algorithm and demand a proof of correctness.

Theorem 15.1 (Correctness of `Prim`) *For every connected graph $G = (V, E)$ and real-valued edge costs, the `Prim` algorithm returns a minimum spanning tree of G.*

See Section 15.4 for a proof of Theorem 15.1.

15.2.3   Straightforward Implementation

As is typical of greedy algorithms, the running time analysis of Prim's algorithm (assuming a straightforward implementation) is far easier than its correctness proof.

Quiz 15.2

Which of the following running times best describes a straightforward implementation of Prim's minimum spanning tree algorithm for graphs in adjacency-list representation? As usual, n and m denote the number of vertices and edges, respectively, of the input graph.

a) $O(m + n)$

b) $O(m \log n)$

c) $O(n^2)$

d) $O(mn)$

(See below for the solution and discussion.)

Correct answer: (d). A straightforward implementation keeps track of which vertices are in X by associating a Boolean variable with each vertex. In each iteration, it performs an exhaustive search through

---

[11]Even a broken analog clock is correct two times a day...

all the edges to identify the cheapest one with one endpoint in each of X and $V - X$. After $n - 1$ iterations, the algorithm runs out of new vertices to add to its set X and halts. Because the number of iterations is $O(n)$ and each takes $O(m)$ time, the overall running time is $O(mn)$.

Proposition 15.2 (Prim Running Time (Straightforward))
For every graph $G = (V, E)$ and real-valued edge costs, the straight-forward implementation of Prim runs in $O(mn)$ time, where $m = |E|$ and $n = |V|$.

*15.3 Speeding Up Prim's Algorithm via Heaps

15.3.1 The Quest for Near-Linear Running Time

The running time of the straightforward implementation of Prim's algorithm (Proposition 15.2) is nothing to sneeze at—it's a polynomial function of the problem size, while exhaustive search through all of a graph's spanning trees can take an exponential amount of time (see footnote 7). This implementation is fast enough to process medium-size graphs (with thousands of vertices and edges) in a reasonable amount of time, but not big graphs (with millions of vertices and edges). Remember the mantra of any algorithm designer worth their salt: Can we do better? The holy grail in algorithm design is a linear-time algorithm (or close to it), and this is what we want for the MST problem.

We don't need a better *algorithm* to achieve a near-linear-time solution to the problem, just a better *implementation* of Prim's algorithm. The key observation is that the straightforward implementation performs minimum computations, over and over, using exhaustive search. Any method for computing repeated minimum computations faster than exhaustive search would translate to a faster implementation of Prim's algorithm.

We mentioned briefly in Section 14.3.6 that there is, in fact, a data structure whose raison d'être is fast minimum computations: the *heap* data structure. Thus, a light bulb should go off in your head: Prim's algorithm calls out for a heap!

15.3.2   The Heap Data Structure

A heap maintains an evolving set of objects with keys and supports several fast operations, of which we'll need three.

Heaps: Three Supported Operations

INSERT: given a heap H and a new object x, add x to H.

EXTRACTMIN: given a heap H, remove and return from H an object with the smallest key (or a pointer to it).

DELETE: given a heap H and a pointer to an object x in H, delete x from H.

For example, if you invoke INSERT four times to add objects with keys 12, 7, 29, and 15 to an empty heap, the EXTRACTMIN operation will return the object with key 7.

Standard implementations of heaps provide the following guarantee.

Theorem 15.3 (Running Time of Three Heap Operations)
In a heap with n objects, the INSERT, EXTRACTMIN, *and* DELETE *operations run in* $O(\log n)$ *time.*

As a bonus, in typical implementations, the constant hidden by the big-O notation and the amount of space overhead are relatively small.[12]

15.3.3   How to Use Heaps in Prim's Algorithm

Heaps enable a blazingly fast, near-linear-time implementation of Prim's algorithm.[13]

---

[12] For the goals of this section, it's not important to know how heaps are implemented and what they look like under the hood. We'll simply be educated clients of them, taking advantage of their logarithmic-time operations. For additional operations and implementation details, see Chapter 10 of *Part 2*.

[13] For readers of *Part 2*, all the ideas in this section will be familiar from the corresponding heap-based implementation of Dijkstra's shortest-path algorithm (Section 10.4).

Theorem 15.4 (Prim Running Time (Heap-Based)) *For every graph $G = (V, E)$ and real-valued edge costs, the heap-based implementation of Prim runs in $O((m + n) \log n)$ time, where $m = |E|$ and $n = |V|$.*[14]

The running time bound in Theorem 15.4 is only a logarithmic factor more than the time required to read the input. The minimum spanning tree problem thus qualifies as a "for-free primitive," joining the likes of sorting, computing the connected components of a graph, and the single-source shortest path problem.

For-Free Primitives

We can think of an algorithm with linear or near-linear running time as a primitive that we can use essentially "for free" because the amount of computation used is barely more than the amount required simply to read the input. When you have a primitive relevant to your problem that is so blazingly fast, why not use it? For example, you can always compute a minimum spanning tree of your undirected graph data in a preprocessing step, even if you're not quite sure how it will help later. One of the goals of this book series is to stock your algorithmic toolbox with as many for-free primitives as possible, ready to be applied at will.

In the heap-based implementation of Prim's algorithm, the objects in the heap correspond to the as-yet-unprocessed vertices ($V - X$ in the Prim pseudocode).[15,16] The key of a vertex $w \in V - X$ is defined as the minimum cost of an incident crossing edge (Figure 15.5).

---

[14]Under our standing assumption that the input graph is connected, m is at least $n - 1$ and we can therefore simplify $O((m + n) \log n)$ to $O(m \log n)$ in the running time bound.

[15]We refer to vertices of the input graph and the corresponding objects in the heap interchangeably.

[16]Your first thought might be to store the *edges* of the input graph in a heap, with an eye toward replacing the minimum computations (over edges) in the straightforward implementation with calls to EXTRACTMIN. This idea can be made to work, but the slicker and quicker implementation stores vertices in a heap.

Invariant

The key of a vertex $w \in V - X$ is the minimum cost of an edge (v, w) with $v \in X$, or $+\infty$ if no such edge exists.

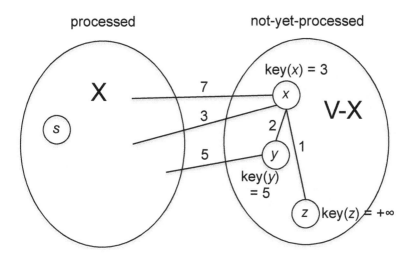

Figure 15.5: The key of a vertex $w \in V - X$ is defined as the minimum cost of an edge (v, w) with $v \in X$ (or $+\infty$, if no such edge exists).

To interpret these keys, imagine using a two-round knockout tournament to identify the minimum-cost edge (v, w) with $v \in X$ and $w \notin X$. The first round comprises a local tournament for each vertex $w \in V - X$, where the participants are the edges (v, w) with $v \in X$ and the first-round winner is the cheapest participant (or $+\infty$, if there are no such edges). The first-round winners (at most one per vertex $w \in V - X$) proceed to the second round, and the final champion is the cheapest first-round winner. Thus, the key of a vertex $w \in V - X$ is exactly the winning edge cost in the local tournament at w. Extracting the vertex with the minimum key then implements the second round of the tournament and returns on a silver platter the next addition to the solution-so-far. As long as we pay the piper and maintain the invariant, keeping objects' keys up to date, we can implement each iteration of Prim's algorithm with a single heap operation.

15.3.4   Pseudocode

The pseudocode then looks like this:

Prim (Heap-Based)

Input: connected undirected graph $G = (V, E)$ in adjacency-list representation and a cost c_e for each edge $e \in E$.

Output: the edges of a minimum spanning tree of G.

```
// Initialization
```
1   $X := \{s\}$, $T = \emptyset$, $H :=$ empty heap
2   **for** every $v \neq s$ **do**
3   **if** there is an edge $(s, v) \in E$ **then**
4           $key(v) := c_{sv}$, $winner(v) := (s, v)$
5   **else**   // v has no crossing incident edges
6           $key(v) := +\infty$, $winner(v) := NULL$
7   INSERT v into H
```
// Main loop
```
8   **while** H is non-empty **do**
9       $w^* :=$ EXTRACTMIN(H)
10   add w^* to X
11   add $winner(w^*)$ to T
```
// update keys to maintain invariant
```
12   **for** every edge (w^*, y) with $y \in V - X$ **do**
13   **if** $c_{w^*y} < key(y)$ **then**
14   DELETE y from H
15              $key(y) := c_{w^*y}$, $winner(y) := (w^*, y)$
16   INSERT y into H
17 **return** T

Each not-yet-processed vertex w records in its *winner* and *key* fields the identity and cost of the winner of its local tournament—the cheapest edge incident to w that crosses the frontier (i.e., edges (v, w) with $v \in X$). Lines 2–7 initialize these values for all the vertices other than s so that the invariant is satisfied and insert these vertices into a heap. Lines 9–11 implement one iteration of the main loop of Prim's algorithm. The invariant ensures that the local winner of the extracted vertex is the cheapest edge crossing the frontier, which is the correct edge to add next to the tree-so-far T. The next quiz illustrates how an extraction can change the frontier, necessitating updates to the keys of vertices still in $V - X$ to maintain the invariant.

Quiz 15.3

In Figure 15.5, suppose the vertex x is extracted and moved to the set X. What should be the new values of y and z's keys, respectively?

a) 1 and 2

b) 2 and 1

c) 5 and $+\infty$

d) $+\infty$ and $+\infty$

(See Section 15.3.6 for the solution and discussion.)

Lines 12–16 of the pseudocode pay the piper and perform the necessary updates to the keys of the vertices remaining in $V - X$. When w^* is moved from $V - X$ to X, edges of the form (w^*, y) with $y \in V - X$ cross the frontier for the first time; these are the new contestants in the local tournaments at the vertices of $V - X$. (We can ignore the fact that edges of the form (u, w^*) with $u \in X$ get sucked into X and no longer cross the frontier, as we're not responsible for maintaining keys for vertices in X.) For a vertex $y \in V - X$, the new winner of its local tournament is either the old winner (stored in $winner(y)$) or the new contestant (w^*, y). Line 12 iterates through the new contestants.[17] Line 13 checks whether an edge (w^*, y) is the new winner in y's local tournament; if it is, lines 14–16 update y's *key* and *winner* fields and the heap H accordingly.[18]

---

[17]This is the main step in which it's so convenient to have the input graph represented via adjacency lists—the edges of the form (w^*, y) can be accessed directly via w^*'s array of incident edges.

[18]Some heap implementations export a DECREASEKEY operation, in which case lines 14–16 can be implemented with one heap operation rather than two.

15.3.5   Running Time Analysis

The initialization phase (lines 1–7) performs $n-1$ heap operations (one INSERT per vertex other than s) and $O(m)$ additional work, where n and m denote the number of vertices and edges, respectively. There are $n-1$ iterations of the main while loop (lines 8–16), so lines 9–11 contribute $O(n)$ heap iterations and $O(n)$ additional work to the overall running time. Bounding the total time spent in lines 12–16 is the tricky part; the key observation is that *each edge of G is examined in line 12 exactly once*, in the iteration in which the first of its endpoints gets sucked into X (i.e., plays the role of w^*). When an edge is examined, the algorithm performs two heap operations (in lines 14 and 16) and $O(1)$ additional work, so the total contribution of lines 12–16 to the running time (over all while loop iterations) is $O(m)$ heap operations plus $O(m)$ additional work. Tallying up, the final scorecard reads

$$O(m+n) \text{ heap operations} + O(m+n) \text{ additional work.}$$

The heap never stores more than $n-1$ objects, so each heap operation runs in $O(\log n)$ time (Theorem 15.3). The overall running time is $O((m+n)\log n)$, as promised by Theorem 15.4. $\mathcal{QED}$

15.3.6   Solution to Quiz 15.3

Correct answer: (b). After the vertex x is moved from $V-X$ to X, the new picture is:

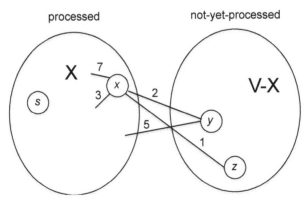

Edges of the form (v,x) with $v \in X$ get sucked into X and no longer cross the frontier (as with the edges with costs 3 and 7). The other edges incident to x, (x, y) and (x, z), get partially yanked out of $V - X$ and now cross the frontier. For both y and z, these new incident crossing edges are cheaper than all their old ones. To maintain the invariant, both of their keys must be updated accordingly: y's key from 5 to 2, and z's key from $+\infty$ to 1.

*15.4   Prim's Algorithm: Proof of Correctness

Proving the correctness of Prim's algorithm (Theorem 15.1) is a bit easier when all the edge costs are distinct. Among friends, let's adopt this assumption for this section. With a little more work, Theorem 15.1 can be proved in its full generality (see Problem 15.5).

The proof breaks down into two steps. The first step identifies a property, called the "minimum bottleneck property," possessed by the output of Prim's algorithm. The second step shows that, in a graph with distinct edge costs, a spanning tree with this property must be a minimum spanning tree.[19]

15.4.1   The Minimum Bottleneck Property

We can motivate the minimum bottleneck property by analogy with Dijkstra's shortest-path algorithm. The only major difference between Prim's and Dijkstra's algorithms is the criterion used to choose a crossing edge in each iteration. Dijkstra's algorithm greedily chooses the eligible edge that minimizes the distance (i.e., the *sum* of edge lengths) from the starting vertex s and, for this reason, computes shortest paths from s to every other vertex (provided edge lengths are nonnegative). Prim's algorithm, by always choosing the eligible edge with minimum individual cost, is effectively striving to minimize the *maximum* edge cost along every path.[20]

---

[19] A popular if more abstract approach to proving the correctness of Prim's (and Kruskal's) algorithm is to use what's known as the "Cut Property" of MSTs; see Problem 15.7 for details.

[20] This observation is related to a mystery that might be troubling readers of *Part 2*: Why is Dijkstra's algorithm correct only with nonnegative edge lengths, while Prim's algorithm is correct with arbitrary (positive or negative) edge costs? A key ingredient in the correctness proof for Dijkstra's algorithm is "path monotonicity," meaning that tacking on additional edges at the end of a path can only make it worse. Tacking a negative-length edge onto a path would decrease its overall length, so nonnegative edge lengths are necessary for path monotonicity.

The minimum bottleneck property makes this idea precise. Given a graph with real-valued edge costs, define the *bottleneck* of a path P as the maximum cost $\max_{e \in P} c_e$ of one of its edges.

The Minimum Bottleneck Property (MBP)

For a graph $G = (V, E)$ with real-valued edge costs, an edge $(v, w) \in E$ satisfies the *minimum bottleneck property (MBP)* if it is a minimum-bottleneck v-w path.

In other words, an edge (v, w) satisfies the MBP if and only if there is no v-w path consisting solely of edges with cost less than c_{vw}. In our running example:

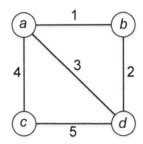

the edge (a, d) does not satisfy the MBP (every edge on the path $a \to b \to d$ is cheaper than (a, d)), nor does the edge (c, d) (every edge on the path $c \to a \to d$ is cheaper than (c, d)). The other three edges do satisfy the MBP, as you should check.[21]

The next lemma implements the first step of our proof plan by relating the output of Prim's algorithm to the MBP.

Lemma 15.5 (Prim Achieves the MBP) *For every connected graph $G = (V, E)$ and real-valued edge costs, every edge chosen by the* Prim *algorithm satisfies the MBP.*

Proof: Consider an edge (v^*, w^*) chosen in an iteration of the Prim algorithm, with $v^* \in X$ and $w^* \in V - X$. By the algorithm's greedy

---

For Prim's algorithm, the relevant measure is the *maximum* cost of an edge in a path, and this measure cannot decrease as additional (positive- or negative-cost) edges are tacked onto the path.

[21] As we'll see, it's no accident that the edges satisfying the MBP in this example are precisely the edges in the minimum spanning tree.

rule,

$$c_{v^*w^*} \le c_{xy} \qquad (15.1)$$

for every edge $(x, y) \in E$ with $x \in X$ and $y \in V - X$.

To prove that (v^*, w^*) satisfies the MBP, consider an arbitrary v^*-w^* path P. Because $v^* \in X$ and $w^* \notin X$, the path P crosses at some point from X to $V - X$, say via the edge (x, y) with $x \in X$ and $y \in V - X$ (Figure 15.6). The bottleneck of P is at least c_{xy}, which by inequality (15.1) is at least $c_{v^*w^*}$. Because P was arbitrary, the edge (v^*, w^*) is a minimum-bottleneck v^*-w^* path. $\mathcal{QED}$

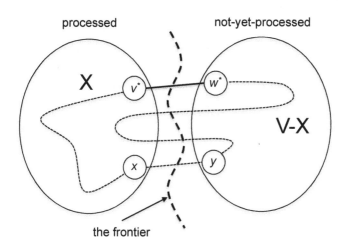

Figure 15.6: Every v^*-w^* path crosses at least once from X to $V - X$. The dotted lines represent one such path.

We set out to solve the minimum spanning tree problem, not to achieve the minimum bottleneck property. But I'd never waste your time; in graphs with distinct edge costs, the latter automatically implies the former.[22]

Theorem 15.6 (MBP Implies MST) *Let $G = (V, E)$ be a graph with distinct real-valued edge costs, and T a spanning tree of G. If every edge of T satisfies the minimum bottleneck property, T is a minimum spanning tree.*

---

[22]The converse of Theorem 15.6 is also true, even with non-distinct edge costs: Every edge of an MST satisfies the MBP (Problem 15.4).

The bad news is that the proof of Theorem 15.6 has several steps. The good news is that we can reuse all of them to also establish the correctness of another important MST algorithm, Kruskal's algorithm (Theorem 15.11 in Section 15.5).[23]

15.4.2 Fun Facts About Spanning Trees

To warm up for the proof of Theorem 15.6, we'll prove some simple and useful facts about undirected graphs and their spanning trees. First, some terminology. A graph $G = (V, E)$—not necessarily connected— naturally falls into "pieces" called the *connected components* of the graph. More formally, a connected component is a maximal subset $S \subseteq V$ of vertices such that there is a path in G from any vertex in S to any other vertex in S. For example, the connected components of the graph in Figure 15.7(a) are $\{1, 3, 5, 7, 9\}$, $\{2, 4\}$, and $\{6, 8, 10\}$. A graph is connected, with a path between every pair of vertices, if and only if it has a single connected component.[24]

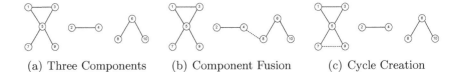

(a) Three Components   (b) Component Fusion   (c) Cycle Creation

Figure 15.7: In (a), a graph with vertex set $\{1, 2, 3, \ldots, 10\}$ and three connected components. In (b), adding the edge $(4, 8)$ fuses two components into one. In (c), adding the edge $(7, 9)$ creates a new cycle.

Now imagine starting from an empty graph (with vertices but no edges) and adding edges to it one by one. What changes when a new edge is added? One possibility is that the new edge fuses two connected components into one (Figure 15.7(b)). We call this a *type-F edge addition* ('F' for "fusion"). Another possibility is that the new edge closes a pre-existing path, creating a cycle (Figure 15.7(c)). We call this a *type-C edge addition* ('C' for "cycle"). Our first lemma

---

[23]Theorem 15.6 does not hold as stated in graphs with non-distinct edge costs. (For a counterexample, consider a triangle with one edge with cost 1 and two edges with cost 2 each.) Nevertheless, Prim's and Kruskal's algorithms remain correct with arbitrary real-valued edge costs (see Problem 15.5).

[24]For more on connected components, including an algorithm to compute them in linear time, see Chapter 8 of *Part 2*.

states that every edge addition (v, w) is either type C or type F (and not both), depending on whether the graph already has a v-w path. If this statement seems obvious to you, feel free to skip the proof and move on.

Lemma 15.7 (Cycle Creation/Component Fusion) *Let $G = (V, E)$ be an undirected graph and $v, w \in V$ two distinct vertices such that $(v, w) \notin E$.*

(a) *(Type C) If v and w are in the same connected component of G, adding the edge (v, w) to G creates at least one new cycle and does not change the number of connected components.*

(b) *(Type F) If v and w are in different connected components of G, adding the edge (v, w) to G does not create any new cycles and decreases the number of connected components by 1.*

Proof: For part (a), if v and w are in the same connected component of G, there is a v-w path P in G. After the edge addition, $P \cup \{(v, w)\}$ forms a new cycle. The connected components remain exactly the same, with the new edge (v, w) swallowed up by the connected component that already contains both its endpoints.

For part (b), let S_1 and S_2 denote the (distinct) connected components of G that contain v and w, respectively. First, after the edge addition, the connected components S_1 and S_2 fuse into a single component $S_1 \cup S_2$, decreasing the number of components by 1. (For vertices $x \in S_1$ and $y \in S_2$, you can produce an x-y path in the new graph by pasting together an x-v path in G, the edge (v, w), and a w-y path in G.) Second, suppose for contradiction that the edge addition *did* create a new cycle C. This cycle must include the new edge (v, w). But then $C - \{(v, w)\}$ would be a v-w path in G, contradicting our assumption that v and w are in different connected components. $\mathcal{QED}$

With Lemma 15.7 at our disposal, we can quickly deduce some interesting facts about spanning trees.

Corollary 15.8 (Spanning Trees Have Exactly $n - 1$ Edges) *Every spanning tree of an n-vertex graph has $n - 1$ edges.*

Proof: Let T be a spanning tree of a graph $G = (V, E)$ with n vertices. Start from the empty graph with vertex set V and add the edges of T one by one. Because T has no cycles, every edge addition is of type F and decreases the number of connected components by 1 (Lemma 15.7):

The process starts with n connected components (with each vertex in its own component) and ends with 1 (because T is a spanning tree), so the number of edge additions must be $n - 1$. *Q.E.D.*

There are two ways a subgraph can fail to be a spanning tree: by containing a cycle or by failing to be connected. A subgraph with $n - 1$ edges—a candidate for a spanning tree, by Corollary 15.8—fails one of the conditions only if it fails both.

Corollary 15.9 (Connectedness and Acyclicity Go Together)
Let $G = (V, E)$ be a graph and $T \subseteq E$ a subset of $n - 1$ edges, where $n = |V|$. The graph (V, T) is connected if and only if it contains no cycles.

Proof: Reprise the edge addition process from Corollary 15.8. If each of the $n - 1$ edge additions has type F, then Lemma 15.7(b) implies that the process concludes with a single connected component and no cycles (i.e., a spanning tree).

Otherwise, there is a type-C edge addition, which by Lemma 15.7(a) creates a cycle and also fails to decrease the number of connected components:

In this case, the process starts with n connected components and the $n - 1$ edge additions decrease the number of connected components at most $n - 2$ times, leaving the final graph (V, T) with at least two connected components. We conclude that (V, T) is neither connected nor acyclic. *Q.E.D.*

We can similarly argue that the output of Prim's algorithm is a spanning tree. (We're not yet claiming that it's a *minimum* spanning tree.)

Corollary 15.10 (Prim Outputs a Spanning Tree) *For   every connected input graph, the* Prim *algorithm outputs a spanning tree.*

Proof: Throughout the algorithm, the vertices of X form one connected component of (V, T) and each vertex of $V - X$ is isolated in its own connected component. Each of the $n - 1$ edge additions involves a vertex w^* of $V - X$ and hence has type F, so the final result is a spanning tree. $\mathcal{QED}$

15.4.3   Proof of Theorem 15.6 (MBP Implies MST)

The proof of Theorem 15.6 is where we use our standing assumption that edges' costs are distinct.

Proof of Theorem 15.6: We proceed by contradiction. Let T be a spanning tree in which every edge satisfies the MBP, and suppose that a minimum spanning tree T^* has a strictly smaller sum of edge costs. Inspired by our proof of Theorem 13.1, the plan is to exchange one edge for another to produce a spanning tree T' with total cost even less than T^*, thereby contradicting the alleged optimality of T^*.

The trees T and T^* must be different and each has $n - 1$ edges, where $n = |V|$ (by Corollary 15.8). Thus, T contains at least one edge $e_1 = (v, w)$ that is not in T^*. Adding e_1 to T^* creates a cycle C that contains e_1 (Lemma 15.7(a)):

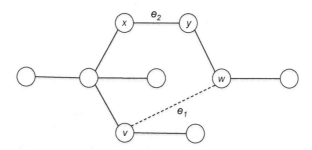

As an edge of T, e_1 satisfies the MBP, so there is at least one edge $e_2 = (x, y)$ in the v-w path $C - \{e_1\}$ with cost at least c_{vw}. Under our assumption that edges' costs are distinct, the cost of e_2 must be strictly larger: $c_{xy} > c_{vw}$.

Now derive T' from $T^* \cup \{e_1\}$ by removing the edge e_2:

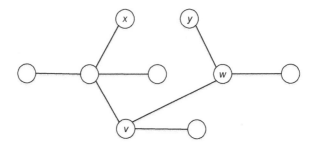

Because T^* has $n - 1$ edges, so does T'. Because T^* is connected, so is T'. (Removing an edge from a cycle undoes a type-C edge addition, which by Lemma 15.7(a) has no effect on the number of connected components.) Corollary 15.9 then implies that T' is also acyclic and hence a spanning tree. Because the cost of e_2 is larger than that of e_1, T' has a lower total cost than T^*; this contradicts the supposed optimality of T^* and completes the proof. $\mathcal{QED}$

15.4.4   Putting It All Together

We now have the ingredients to immediately deduce the correctness of Prim's algorithm in graphs with distinct edge costs.

Proof of Theorem 15.1: Corollary 15.10 proves that the output of Prim's algorithm is a spanning tree. Lemma 15.5 implies that every edge of this spanning tree satisfies the MBP. Theorem 15.6 guarantees that this spanning tree is a minimum spanning tree. $\mathcal{QED}$

15.5   Kruskal's Algorithm

This section describes a second algorithm for the minimum spanning tree problem, *Kruskal's algorithm*.[25] With our blazingly fast heap-based implementation of Prim's algorithm, why should we care about

---

[25]Discovered by Joseph B. Kruskal in the mid-1950s—roughly the same time that Prim and Dijkstra were rediscovering what is now called Prim's algorithm.

Kruskal's algorithm? Three reasons. One, it's a first-ballot hall-of-fame algorithm, so every seasoned programmer and computer scientist should know about it. Properly implemented, it is competitive with Prim's algorithm in both theory and practice. Two, it provides an opportunity to study a new and useful data structure, the *disjoint-set* or *union-find* data structure. Three, there are some very cool connections between Kruskal's algorithm and widely-used clustering algorithms (see Section 15.8).

15.5.1   Example

As with Prim's algorithm, it's helpful to see an example of Kruskal's algorithm in action before proceeding to its pseudocode. Here's the input graph:

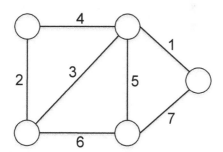

Kruskal's algorithm, like Prim's algorithm, greedily constructs a spanning tree one edge at a time. But rather than growing a single tree from a starting vertex, Kruskal's algorithm can grow multiple trees in parallel, content for them to coalesce into a single tree only at the end of the algorithm. So, while Prim's algorithm was constrained to choose the cheapest edge crossing the current frontier, Kruskal's algorithm is free to choose the cheapest remaining edge in the entire graph. Well, not quite: Cycles are a no-no, so it chooses the cheapest edge that doesn't create a cycle.

In our example, Kruskal's algorithm starts with an empty edge set T and, in its first iteration, greedily considers the cheapest edge (the edge of cost 1) and adds it to T. The second iteration follows suit with the next-cheapest edge (the edge of cost 2). At this point, the solution-so-far T looks like:

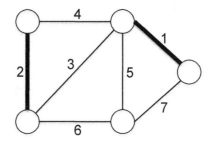

The two edges chosen so far are disjoint, so the algorithm is effectively growing two trees in parallel. The next iteration considers the edge with cost 3. Its inclusion does not create a cycle and also happens to fuse the two trees-so-far into one:

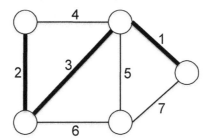

The algorithm next considers the edge of cost 4. Adding this edge to T would create a cycle (with the edges of cost 2 and 3), so the algorithm is forced to skip it. The next-best option is the edge of cost 5; its inclusion does not create a cycle and, in fact, results in a spanning tree:

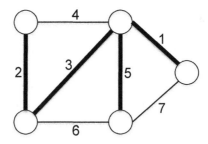

The algorithm skips the edge of cost 6 (which would create a triangle with the edges of cost 3 and 5) as well as the final edge, of cost 7 (which would create a triangle with the edges of cost 1 and 5). The final output above is the minimum spanning tree of the graph (as you should check).

15.5.2   Pseudocode

With our intuition solidly in place, the following pseudocode won't surprise you.

Kruskal

Input: connected undirected graph $G = (V, E)$ in adjacency-list representation and a cost c_e for each edge $e \in E$.

Output: the edges of a minimum spanning tree of G.

```
// Preprocessing
```
$T := \emptyset$
sort edges of E by cost   // e.g., using MergeSort[26]
```
// Main loop
```
for each $e \in E$, in nondecreasing order of cost **do**
    if $T \cup \{e\}$ is acyclic **then**
        $T := T \cup \{e\}$
return T

Kruskal's algorithm considers the edges of the input graph one by one, from cheapest to most expensive, so it makes sense to sort them in nondecreasing order of cost in a preprocessing step (using your favorite sorting algorithm; see footnote 3 in Chapter 13). Ties between edges can be broken arbitrarily. The main loop zips through the edges in this order, adding an edge to the solution-so-far provided it doesn't create a cycle.[27]

It's not obvious that the Kruskal algorithm returns a spanning tree, let alone a minimum one. But it does!

Theorem 15.11 (Correctness of Kruskal) *For every connected graph $G = (V, E)$ and real-valued edge costs, the Kruskal algorithm returns a minimum spanning tree of G.*

---

[26]The abbreviation "e.g." stands for *exempli gratia* and means "for example."

[27]One easy optimization: You can stop the algorithm early once $|V| - 1$ edges have been added to T, as at this point T is already a spanning tree (by Corollary 15.9).

We've already done most of the heavy lifting in our correctness proof for Prim's algorithm (Theorem 15.1). Section 15.7 supplies the remaining details of the proof of Theorem 15.11.

15.5.3 Straightforward Implementation

How would you actually implement Kruskal's algorithm and, in particular, the cycle-checking required in each iteration?

Quiz 15.4

Which of the following running times best describes a straightforward implementation of Kruskal's MST algorithm for graphs in adjacency-list representation? As usual, n and m denote the number of vertices and edges, respectively, of the input graph.

 a) $O(m \log n)$

 b) $O(n^2)$

 c) $O(mn)$

 d) $O(m^2)$

(See below for the solution and discussion.)

Correct answer: (c). In the preprocessing step, the algorithm sorts the edge array of the input graph, which has m entries. With a good sorting algorithm (like MergeSort), this step contributes $O(m \log n)$ work to the overall running time.[28] This work will be dominated by that done by the main loop of the algorithm, which we analyze next.

The main loop has m iterations. Each iteration is responsible for checking whether the edge $e = (v, w)$ under examination can be added to the solution-so-far T without creating a cycle. By Lemma 15.7,

---

[28] Why $O(m \log n)$ instead of $O(m \log m)$? Because there's no difference between the two expressions. The number of edges of an n-vertex connected graph with no parallel edges is at least $n - 1$ (achieved by a tree) and at most $\binom{n}{2} = \frac{n(n-1)}{2}$ (achieved by a complete graph). Thus $\log m$ lies between $\log(n - 1)$ and $2 \log n$ for every connected graph with no parallel edges, which justifies using $\log m$ and $\log n$ interchangeably inside a big-O expression.

adding e to T creates a cycle if and only if T already contains a v-w path. The latter condition can be checked in linear time using any reasonable graph search algorithm, like breadth- or depth-first search starting from v (see Chapter 8 of *Part 2*). And by "linear time," we mean linear in the size of the graph (V, T) which, as an acyclic graph with n vertices, has at most $n - 1$ edges. The per-iteration running time is therefore $O(n)$, for an overall running time of $O(mn)$.

Proposition 15.12 (Kruskal Run Time (Straightforward))
For every graph $G = (V, E)$ and real-valued edge costs, the straightforward implementation of Kruskal *runs in $O(mn)$ time, where $m = |E|$ and $n = |V|$.*

*15.6   Speeding Up Kruskal's Algorithm via Union-Find

As with Prim's algorithm, we can reduce the running time of Kruskal's algorithm from the reasonable polynomial bound of $O(mn)$ (Proposition 15.12) to the blazingly fast near-linear bound of $O(m \log n)$ through the deft use of a data structure. None of the data structures discussed previously in this book series are right for the job; we'll need a new one, called the *union-find* data structure.[29]

Theorem 15.13 (Kruskal Run Time (Union-Find-Based))
For every graph $G = (V, E)$ and real-valued edge costs, the union-find-based implementation of Kruskal *runs in $O((m + n) \log n)$ time, where $m = |E|$ and $n = |V|$.*[30]

15.6.1   The Union-Find Data Structure

Whenever a program does a significant computation over and over again, it's a clarion call for a data structure to speed up those computations. Prim's algorithm performs minimum computations in each iteration of its main loop, so the heap data structure is an obvious match. Each iteration of Kruskal's algorithm performs a cycle check or, equivalently, a path check. (Adding an edge (v, w) to the solution-so-far T creates a cycle if and only if T already contains a v-w path.)

---
[29] Also known as the *disjoint-set* data structure.

[30] Again, under our standing assumption that the input graph is connected, we can simplify the $O((m + n) \log n)$ bound to $O(m \log n)$.

What kind of data structure would allow us to quickly identify whether
the solution-so-far contains a path between a given pair of vertices?

The raison d'être of the union-find data structure is to maintain
a partition of a static set of objects.[31] In the initial partition, each
object is in its own set. These sets can merge over time, but they can
never split:

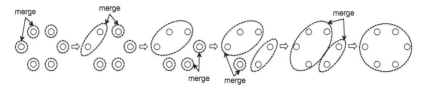

In our application of speeding up Kruskal's algorithm, the objects
will correspond to the vertices of the input graph and the sets in the
partition to the connected components of the solution-so-far T:

Checking whether T already contains a v-w path then boils down to
checking whether v and w belong to the same set of the partition (i.e.,
to the same connected component).

The union-find data structure supports two operations for access-
ing and modifying its partition, the—wait for it—UNION and FIND
operations.

Union-Find: Supported Operations

INITIALIZE: given an array X of objects, create a union-find
data structure with each object $x \in X$ in its own set.

FIND: given a union-find data structure and an object x in
it, return the name of the set that contains x.

UNION: given a union-find data structure and two objects
$x, y \in X$ in it, merge the sets that contain x and y into a

---

[31]A *partition* of a set X of objects is a way of splitting them into one or more
groups. More formally, it is a collection $S_1, S_2, \ldots, S_p$ of non-empty subsets of X
such that each object $x \in X$ belongs to exactly one of the subsets.

single set.[32]

With a good implementation, the UNION and FIND operations both take time logarithmic in the number of objects.[33]

Theorem 15.14 (Running Time of Union-Find Operations)
In a union-find data structure with n objects, the INITIALIZE, FIND, and UNION operations run in $O(n)$, $O(\log n)$, and $O(\log n)$ time, respectively.

Summarizing, here's the scorecard:

Operation	Running time
INITIALIZE	$O(n)$
FIND	$O(\log n)$
UNION	$O(\log n)$

Table 15.1: The union-find data structure: supported operations and their running times, where n denotes the number of objects.

We first show how to implement Kruskal's algorithm given a union-find data structure with logarithmic-time operations, and then outline an implementation of such a data structure.

15.6.2   Pseudocode

The main idea for speeding up Kruskal's algorithm is to use a union-find data structure to keep track of the connected components of the solution-so-far. Each vertex is in its own connected component at the beginning of the algorithm and, accordingly, a union-find data structure is born with each object in a different set. Whenever a new edge (v, w) is added to the solution-so-far, the connected components of v and w fuse into one, and one UNION operation suffices to update

---

[32]If x and y are already in the same set of the partition, this operation has no effect.

[33]These bounds are for the quick-and-dirty implementation in Section 15.6.4. There are better implementations but they are overkill for the present application. See the bonus videos at www.algorithmsilluminated.org for an in-depth look at state-of-the-art union-find data structures. (Highlights include "union-by-rank," "path compression," and the "inverse Ackermann function." It's amazing stuff!)

the union-find data structure accordingly. Checking whether an edge addition (v, w) would create a cycle is equivalent to checking whether v and w are already in the same connected component. This reduces to two FIND operations.

Kruskal (Union-Find-Based)

Input: connected undirected graph $G = (V, E)$ in adjacency-list representation and a cost c_e for each edge $e \in E$.

Output: the edges of a minimum spanning tree of G.

```
// Initialization
T := ∅
U := INITIALIZE(V)   // union-find data structure
sort edges of E by cost   // e.g., using MergeSort
// Main loop
for each (v, w) ∈ E, in nondecreasing order of cost do
    if FIND(U, v) ≠ FIND(U, w) then
        // no v-w path in T, so OK to add (v, w)
        T := T ∪ {(v, w)}
        // update due to component fusion
        UNION(U, v, w)
return T
```

The algorithm maintains the invariant that, at the beginning of a loop iteration, the sets of the union-find data structure U correspond to the connected components of (V, T). Thus, the condition $\text{FIND}(U, v) \neq \text{FIND}(U, w)$ is met if and only if v and w are in different connected components of (V, T), or equivalently, if and only if adding (v, w) to T does not create a cycle. We conclude that the union-find-based implementation of Kruskal is faithful to its original implementation, with both versions producing the same output.

15.6.3   Running Time Analysis

The running time analysis of the union-find-based implementation of Kruskal's algorithm is straightforward. Initializing the union-find data structure takes $O(n)$ time. As in the original implementation, the sorting step requires $O(m \log n)$ time (see Quiz 15.4). There are m iterations of the main loop and each uses two FIND operations (for a total of $2m$). There is one UNION operation for each edge added to the output which, as an acyclic graph, has at most $n - 1$ edges (Corollary 15.8). Provided the FIND and UNION operations run in $O(\log n)$ time, as assured by Theorem 15.14, the total running time is:

preprocessing	$O(n) + O(m \log n)$
$2m$ FIND operations	$O(m \log n)$
$n - 1$ UNION operations	$O(n \log n)$
+ remaining bookkeeping	$O(m)$
total	$O((m + n) \log n)$.

This matches the running time bound promised in Theorem 15.13. *QED*

15.6.4   Quick-and-Dirty Implementation of Union-Find

The Parent Graph

Under the hood, a union-find data structure is implemented as an array and can be visualized as a collection of directed trees. The array has one position for each object $x \in X$. Each array entry has a *parent* field that stores the array index of some object $y \in X$ (with $y = x$ allowed). We can then picture the current state of the data structure as a directed graph—the *parent graph*—with vertices corresponding to (indices of) objects $x \in X$ and a directed edge (x, y), called a *parent edge*, whenever $parent(x) = y$.[34] For example, if X has six objects and the current state of the data structure is:

Index of object x	$parent(x)$
1	4
2	1
3	1
4	4
5	6
6	6

then the parent graph is a pair of disjoint trees, with each root pointing back to itself:

---

[34]The parent graph exists only in our minds. Do not confuse it with the actual (undirected) input graph in Kruskal's algorithm.

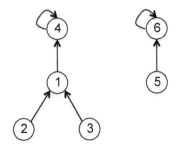

In general, the sets in the partition maintained by the data structure will correspond to the trees in the parent graph, with each set inheriting the name of its root object. The trees are not necessarily binary, as there is no limit to the number of objects that can have the same parent. In the example above, the first four objects belong to a set named "4," and the last two to a set named "6."

INITIALIZE and FIND

The intended semantics of the parent graph already dictate how the INITIALIZE and FIND operations should be implemented.

INITIALIZE

1. For each $i = 1, 2, \ldots, n$, initialize $parent(i)$ to i.

The INITIALIZE operation clearly runs in $O(n)$ time. The initial parent graph consists of isolated vertices with self-loops:

For the FIND operation, we leap from parent to parent until we arrive at a root object, which can be identified by its self-loop.

FIND

1. Starting from x's position in the array, repeatedly traverse parent edges until reaching a position j with $parent(j) = j$.

2. Return j.

If FIND is invoked for the third object in our running example (page 86), the operation checks position 3 (with $parent(3) = 1$), then position 1 (with $parent(1) = 4$), and finally returns the position 4 (a root, as $parent(4) = 4$).

Define the *depth* of an object x as the number of parent edge traversals performed by FIND from x. In our running example, the fourth and sixth objects have depth 0, the first and fifth objects have depth 1, and the second and third objects have depth 2. The FIND operation performs $O(1)$ work per parent edge traversal, so its worst-case running time is proportional to the largest depth of any object—equivalently, to the largest *height* of one of the trees in the parent graph.

Quiz 15.5

What's the running time of the FIND operation, as a function of the number n of objects?

  a) $O(1)$

  b) $O(\log n)$

  c) $O(n)$

  d) Not enough information to answer

(See Section 15.6.5 for the solution and discussion.)

UNION

When the UNION operation is invoked with objects x and y, the two trees T_1 and T_2 of the parent graph containing them must be merged into a single tree. The simplest solution is to demote the root of one of the trees and promote that of the other. For example, if we choose to demote T_1's root, it is installed as a child of an object in the other tree T_2, meaning its *parent* field is reassigned from its own array index to that of an object in T_2. The promoted root (from T_2) continues to serve as the root of the merged tree. There are several ways to fuse the two trees in this way, such as:

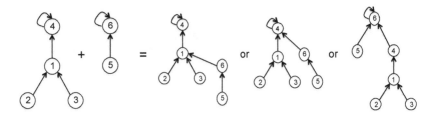

To complete the implementation, we must make two decisions:

1. Which of the two roots do we promote?

2. Under which object do we install the demoted root?

Suppose we install the root of a tree T_1 under an object z of another tree T_2. What are the consequences for the running time of a FIND operation? For an object in T_2, none: The operation traverses exactly the same set of parent edges as before. For an object x that previously inhabited T_1, the FIND operation traverses the same path as before (from x to the old root r of T_1), plus the new parent edge from r to z, plus the parent edges from z to the root of T_2:

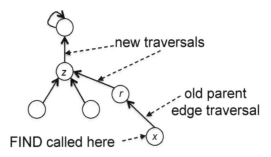

That is, the depth of every object in T_1 increases by 1 (for the new parent edge) plus the depth of z.

The answer to the second question is now clear: Install the demoted root directly under the (depth-0) promoted root so that the occupants of T_1 suffer a depth increase of only 1.

Quiz 15.6

Suppose we arbitrarily choose which root to promote. What's the running time of the FIND operation as a function of the number n of objects?

---

a) $O(1)$

b) $O(\log n)$

c) $O(n)$

d) Not enough information to answer

(See Section 15.6.5 for the solution and discussion.)

The solution to Quiz 15.6 demonstrates that, to achieve the desired logarithmic running time, we need another idea. If we demote the root of T_1, then T_1's occupants are pushed one step further from the new root; otherwise, T_2's occupants suffer the same fate. It seems only fair to minimize the number of objects suffering a depth increase, which means we should demote the root of the smaller tree (breaking ties arbitrarily).[35] To pull this off, we need easy access to the populations of the two trees. So, along with the *parent* field, the data structure stores with each array entry a *size* field, initialized to 1 in INITIALIZE. When two trees are merged, the *size* field of the promoted root is updated accordingly, to the combined size of the two trees.[36]

UNION

1. Invoke FIND twice to locate the positions i and j of the roots of the parent graph trees that contain x and y, respectively. If $i = j$, return.

2. If $size(i) \geq size(j)$, set $parent(j) := i$ and $size(i) := size(i) + size(j)$.

3. If $size(i) < size(j)$, set $parent(i) := j$ and $size(j) := size(i) + size(j)$.

In our running example (page 86), this implementation of UNION promotes the root 4 and demotes the root 6, resulting in:

---

[35]This implementation choice goes by the name *union-by-size*. Another good idea is *union-by-rank*, which demotes the root of the tree with the smaller height (breaking ties arbitrarily). Union-by-rank is discussed at length in the bonus videos at www.algorithmsilluminated.org.

[36]There is no need to keep the *size* field accurate after a root has been demoted to a non-root.

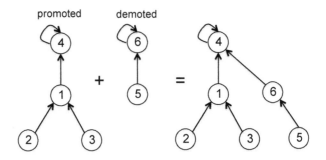

A UNION operation performs two FIND operations and $O(1)$ additional work, so its running time matches that of FIND. Which is...?

Quiz 15.7

With the implementation of UNION above, what's the running time of the FIND (and, hence, UNION) operation, as a function of the number n of objects?

a) $O(1)$

b) $O(\log n)$

c) $O(n)$

d) Not enough information to answer

(See Section 15.6.5 for the solution and discussion.)

With the solution to Quiz 15.7, we conclude that our quick-and-dirty implementation of a union-find data structure fulfills the running time guarantees promised by Theorem 15.14 and Table 15.1.

15.6.5   Solutions to Quizzes 15.5–15.7

Solution to Quiz 15.5

Correct answer: (c or d). The worst-case running time of FIND is proportional to the biggest height of a tree of the parent graph. How big can this be? The answer depends on how we implement the UNION operation; in this sense, answer (d) is correct. A poor implementation can lead to a tree with height as large as $n - 1$:

In this sense, answer (c) is also correct.

Solution to Quiz 15.6

Correct answer: (c). With arbitrary promotion and demotion decisions, a sequence of $n - 1$ UNION operations can produce the height-$(n - 1)$ tree shown in the solution to Quiz 15.5, with each operation installing the tree-so-far underneath a previously isolated object.

Solution to Quiz 15.7

Correct answer: (b). Every object x begins with depth 0. Only one type of event can increment x's depth: a UNION operation in which the root of x's tree in the parent graph gets demoted. By our promotion criterion, this happens only when x's tree is merged with another tree that is at least as big. In other words:

> *whenever x's depth is incremented, the population of x's tree at least doubles.*

Because the population cannot exceed the total number n of objects, the depth of x cannot be incremented more than $\log_2 n$ times. Because the running time of FIND is proportional to the depth of an object, its worst-case running time is $O(\log n)$.

*15.7 Kruskal's Algorithm: Proof of Correctness

This section proves the correctness of Kruskal's algorithm (Theorem 15.11) under the assumption that edges' costs are distinct. Theorem 15.11 can be proved in its full generality with a bit more work (see Problem 15.5).

The first order of business is to show that the algorithm's output is connected (and, as it's clearly acyclic, a spanning tree). To this end, the next lemma shows that once an edge (v, w) is processed by Kruskal, the solution-so-far (and, hence, the final output) necessarily contains a v-w path.

Lemma 15.15 (Connecting Adjacent Vertices) *Let T be the set of edges chosen by Kruskal up to and including the iteration that examines the edge $e = (v, w)$. Then, v and w are in the same connected component of the graph (V, T).*

Proof: In the terminology of Lemma 15.7, adding e to the solution-so-far is either a type-C or type-F edge addition. In the first case, v and w already belong to the same connected component prior to e's examination. In the second case, the algorithm will add the edge (v, w) to its solution-so-far (by Lemma 15.7(b), this doesn't create a cycle), directly connecting v and w and fusing their connected components into one. $\mathcal{QED}$

The following corollary extends Lemma 15.15 from individual edges to multi-hop paths.

Corollary 15.16 (From Edges to Paths) *Let P be a v-w path in G, and T the set of edges chosen by Kruskal up to and including the last iteration that examines an edge of P. Then, v and w are in the same connected component of the graph (V, T).*

Proof: Denote the edges of P by $(x_0, x_1), (x_1, x_2), \ldots, (x_{p-1}, x_p)$, where x_0 is v and x_p is w. By Lemma 15.15, immediately after the iteration that processes the edge (x_{i-1}, x_i), x_{i-1} and x_i lie in the same connected component of the solution-so-far. This remains true as more edges are included in subsequent iterations. After all the edges of P have been processed, all its vertices—and, in particular, its endpoints v and w—belong to the same connected component of the solution-so-far (V, T). $\mathcal{QED}$

The next step argues that Kruskal outputs a spanning tree.

Lemma 15.17 (Kruskal Outputs a Spanning Tree) *For every connected input graph, the Kruskal algorithm outputs a spanning tree.*

Proof: The algorithm explicitly ensures that its final output T is acyclic. To prove that its output is also connected, we can argue that all its vertices belong to the same connected component of (V, T). Fix a pair v, w of vertices; because the input graph is connected, it contains a v-w path P. By Corollary 15.16, once the Kruskal algorithm has processed every edge of P, its endpoints v and w belong to the same connected component of the solution-so-far (and, hence, of the final output (V, T)). $\mathcal{QED}$

To apply Theorem 15.6, we must prove that every edge chosen by the Kruskal algorithm satisfies the minimum bottleneck property (MBP).[37]

Lemma 15.18 (Kruskal Achieves the MBP) *For every connected graph $G = (V, E)$ and real-valued edge costs, every edge chosen by the Kruskal algorithm satisfies the MBP.*

Proof: We prove the contrapositive, that the output of Kruskal never includes an edge that fails to satisfy the MBP. Let $e = (v, w)$ be such an edge, and P a v-w path in G in which every edge has cost less than c_e. Because Kruskal scans through the edges in order of nondecreasing cost, the algorithm processes every edge of P before e. Corollary 15.16 now implies that, by the time Kruskal reaches the edge e, its endpoints v and w already belong to the same connected component of the solution-so-far T. Adding e to T would create a cycle (Lemma 15.7(a)), so Kruskal excludes the edge from its output. $\mathcal{QED}$

Putting it all together proves Theorem 15.11 for graphs with distinct edge costs:

Proof of Theorem 15.11: Lemma 15.17 proves that the output of Kruskal's algorithm is a spanning tree. Lemma 15.18 implies that every edge of this spanning tree satisfies the MBP. Theorem 15.6 guarantees that this spanning tree is a minimum spanning tree. $\mathcal{QED}$

---

[37]Recall from Section 15.4 that an edge $e = (v, w)$ in a graph G satisfies the MBP if and only if every v-w path in G has an edge with cost at least c_e.

15.8   Application: Single-Link Clustering

Unsupervised learning is a branch of machine learning and statistics
that strives to understand large collections of data points by finding
hidden patterns in them. Each data point could represent a person,
an image, a document, a genome sequence, and so on. For example, a data point corresponding to a 100-by-100 pixel color image
might be a 30000-dimensional vector, with 3 coordinates per pixel
recording the intensities of red, green, and blue in that pixel.[38] This
section highlights a connection between one of the most basic algorithms in unsupervised learning and Kruskal's minimum spanning
tree algorithm.

15.8.1   Clustering

One widely-used approach to unsupervised learning is *clustering*, in
which the goal is to partition the data points into "coherent groups"
(called *clusters*) of "similar points" (Figure 15.8). To make this more
precise, suppose we have a *similarity function* f that assigns a nonnegative real number to each pair of data points. We assume that f
is *symmetric*, meaning $f(x, y) = f(y, x)$ for every pair x, y of data
points. We can then interpret points x, y with a small value of $f(x, y)$
as "similar," and those with a large value as "dissimilar."[39] For example, if the data points are vectors with a common dimension, like in
the image example above, $f(x, y)$ could be defined as the Euclidean
(i.e., straight-line) distance between x and y.[40] For another example,
Section 17.1 defines *Needleman-Wunsch distance*, which is a symmetric similarity function designed for genome sequences. In an ideal
clustering, data points in the same cluster are relatively similar while
those in different clusters are relatively dissimilar.

Let k denote the number of clusters desired. Sensible values for k
range from 2 to a large number, depending on the application. For

---

[38]*Supervised* learning focuses on prediction rather than pattern-finding per
se. Here, each data point also has a label (e.g., 1 if the image is of a cat and 0
otherwise), and the goal is to accurately predict the labels of as-yet-unseen data
points.

[39]With these semantics, it's arguably more accurate to call f a *dissimilarity*
function.

[40]If $x = (x_1, x_2, \ldots, x_d)$ and $y = (y_1, y_2, \ldots, y_d)$ are d-dimensional vectors, the
precise formula is $f(x, y) = \sqrt{\sum_{i=1}^{d}(x_i - y_i)^2}$.

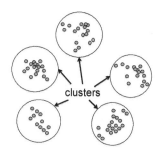

clusters

Figure 15.8: In an ideal clustering, data points in the same cluster are relatively similar while those in different clusters are relatively dissimilar.

example, if the goal is to cluster blog posts about U.S. politics into groups of "left-leaning" and "right-leaning" posts, it makes sense to choose $k = 2$. If the goal is to cluster a diverse collection of images according to their subject, a larger value of k should be used. When unsure about the best value for k, you can try several different choices and select your favorite among the resulting partitions.

15.8.2   Bottom-Up Clustering

The main idea in *bottom-up* or *agglomerative* clustering is to begin with every data point in its own cluster, and then successively merge pairs of clusters until exactly k remain.

Bottom-Up Clustering (Generic)

Input: a set X of data points, a symmetric similarity function f, and a positive integer $k \in \{1, 2, 3, \ldots, |X|\}$.
Output: a partition of X into k non-empty sets.

$C := \emptyset$ // keeps track of current clusters
for each $x \in X$ **do**
     add $\{x\}$ to C // each point in own cluster
// Main loop
while C contains more than k clusters **do**
     remove clusters S_1, S_2 from C // details TBA
     add $S_1 \cup S_2$ to C // merge clusters
return C

Each iteration of the main loop decreases the number of clusters in C by 1, so there are a total of $|X| - k$ iterations (Figure 15.9).[41]

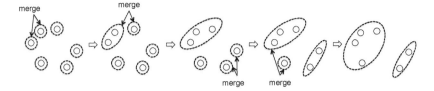

Figure 15.9: In bottom-up clustering, each point begins in its own cluster and pairs of clusters are successively merged until only k clusters remain.

Our generic bottom-up clustering algorithm does not specify which pair of clusters to merge in each iteration. Can we use a greedy approach? If so, greedy with respect to what criterion?

The next step is to derive a similarity function F for pairs of clusters from the given function f for pairs of data points. For example, one of the simplest choices for F is the best-case similarity between points in the different clusters:

$$F(S_1, S_2) = \min_{x \in S_1, y \in S_2} f(x, y). \tag{15.2}$$

Other reasonable choices for F include the worst-case or average similarity between points in the different clusters. In any case, once the function F is chosen, the generic bottom-up clustering algorithm can be specialized to greedily merge the "most similar" pair of clusters in each iteration:

Bottom-Up Clustering (Greedy)

// Main loop
while C contains more than k clusters **do**
    remove from C the clusters S_1, S_2 that minimize
    $F(S_1, S_2)$ // e.g., with F as in (15.2)
    add $S_1 \cup S_2$ to C
return C

---

[41]Bottom-up clustering is only one of several common approaches to clustering. For example, *top-down* algorithms begin with all the data points in a single cluster and successively split clusters in two until there are exactly k clusters. Other algorithms, like *k-means clustering*, maintain k clusters from beginning to end.

Single-link clustering refers to greedy bottom-up clustering with the best-case similarity function (15.2). Do you see any connections between single-link clustering and Kruskal's minimum spanning tree algorithm (Section 15.5)? Take some time to think about it.

*   *   *   *   *   *   *   *   *   *   *

Kruskal's algorithm begins with the empty edge set and each vertex isolated in its own connected component, just as single-link clustering begins with each data point in its own cluster. Each iteration of Kruskal's algorithm that adds a new edge fuses two connected components into one, just as each iteration of single-link clustering merges two clusters into one. Kruskal's algorithm repeatedly adds the cheapest new edge that does not create a cycle, fusing the components containing its endpoints, just as single-link clustering repeatedly merges the pair of clusters containing the most similar pair of data points in different clusters. Thus, Kruskal's algorithm corresponds to single-link clustering, with vertices substituting for data points and connected components for clusters. The one difference is that single-link clustering stops once there are k clusters, while Kruskal's algorithm continues until only one connected component remains. We conclude that *single-link clustering is the same as Kruskal's algorithm, stopped early.*

Single-Link Clustering via Kruskal's Algorithm

1. Define a complete undirected graph $G = (X, E)$ from the data set X and similarity function f, with vertex set X and one edge $(x, y) \in E$ with cost $c_{xy} = f(x, y)$ for each vertex pair $x, y \in X$.

2. Run Kruskal's algorithm with the input graph G until the solution-so-far T contains $|X| - k$ edges or, equivalently, until the graph (X, T) has k connected components.

3. Compute the connected components of (X, T) and return the corresponding partition of X.

The Upshot

☆ A spanning tree of a graph is an acyclic subgraph that contains a path between each pair of vertices.

☆ In the minimum spanning tree (MST) problem, the input is a connected undirected graph with real-valued edge costs and the goal is to compute a spanning tree with the minimum-possible sum of edge costs.

☆ Prim's algorithm constructs an MST one edge at a time, starting from an arbitrary vertex and growing like a mold until the entire vertex set is spanned. In each iteration, it greedily chooses the cheapest edge that expands the reach of the solution-so-far.

☆ When implemented with a heap data structure, Prim's algorithm runs in $O(m \log n)$ time, where m and n denote the number of edges and vertices of the input graph, respectively.

☆ Kruskal's algorithm also constructs an MST one edge at a time, greedily choosing the cheapest edge whose addition does not create a cycle in the solution-so-far.

☆ When implemented with a union-find data structure, Kruskal's algorithm runs in $O(m \log n)$ time.

☆ The first step in the proofs of correctness for Prim's and Kruskal's algorithms is to show that each algorithm chooses only edges satisfying the minimum bottleneck property (MBP).

☆ The second step is to use an exchange argument to prove that a spanning tree in which every edge satisfies the MBP must be an MST.

☆ Single-link clustering is a greedy bottom-up clustering method in unsupervised learning and it corresponds to Kruskal's algorithm, stopped early.

Test Your Understanding

Problem 15.1 *(H)* Consider an undirected graph $G = (V, E)$ in which every edge $e \in E$ has a distinct and nonnegative cost. Let T be an MST and P a shortest path from some vertex s to some other vertex t. Now suppose the cost of every edge e of G is increased by 1 and becomes $c_e + 1$. Call this new graph G'. Which of the following is true about G'?

a) T must be an MST and P must be a shortest s-t path.

b) T must be an MST but P may not be a shortest s-t path.

c) T may not be an MST but P must be a shortest s-t path.

d) T may not be an MST and P may not be a shortest s-t path.

Problem 15.2 *(H)* Consider the following algorithm that attempts to compute an MST of a connected undirected graph $G = (V, E)$ with distinct edge costs by running Kruskal's algorithm "in reverse":

Kruskal (**Reverse Version**)

$T := E$
sort edges of E in decreasing order of cost
for each $e \in E$, in order **do**
    if $T - \{e\}$ is connected **then**
        $T := T - \{e\}$
return T

Which of the following statements is true?

a) The output of the algorithm will never have a cycle, but it might not be connected.

b) The output of the algorithm will always be connected, but it might have cycles.

c) The algorithm always outputs a spanning tree, but it might not be an MST.

d) The algorithm always outputs an MST.

Problem 15.3 *(H)* Which of the following problems reduce, in a straightforward way, to the minimum spanning tree problem? (Choose all that apply.)

a) The maximum-cost spanning tree problem. That is, among all spanning trees T of a connected graph with edge costs, compute one with the maximum-possible sum $\sum_{e \in T} c_e$ of edge costs.

b) The minimum-product spanning tree problem. That is, among all spanning trees T of a connected graph with strictly positive edge costs, compute one with the minimum-possible product $\prod_{e \in T} c_e$ of edge costs.

c) The single-source shortest-path problem. In this problem, the input comprises a connected undirected graph $G = (V, E)$, a nonnegative length ℓ_e for each edge $e \in E$, and a designated starting vertex $s \in V$. The required output is, for every possible destination $v \in V$, the minimum total length of a path from s to v.

d) Given a connected undirected graph $G = (V, E)$ with positive edge costs, compute a minimum-cost set $F \subseteq E$ of edges such that the graph $(V, E - F)$ is acyclic.

On Reductions

A problem A *reduces* to a problem B if an algorithm that solves B can be easily translated into one that solves A. For example, the problem of computing the median element of an array reduces to the problem of sorting the array. Reductions are one of the most important concepts in the study of algorithms and their limitations, and they can also have great practical utility.

You should always be on the lookout for reductions. Whenever you encounter a seemingly new problem, always ask: Is the problem a disguised version of one you already know how to solve? Alternatively, can you reduce the general version of the problem to a special case?

Challenge Problems

Problem 15.4 *(S)* Prove the converse of Theorem 15.6: If T is an MST of a graph with real-valued edge costs, every edge of T satisfies the minimum bottleneck property.

Problem 15.5 *(S)* Prove the correctness of Prim's and Kruskal's algorithms (Theorems 15.1 and 15.11) in full generality, for graphs in which edges' costs need not be distinct.

Problem 15.6 *(H)* Prove that in a connected undirected graph with distinct edge costs, there is a unique MST.

Problem 15.7 *(S)* An alternative approach to proving the correctness of Prim's and Kruskal's algorithms is to use what's called the *Cut Property* of MSTs. Assume throughout this problem that edges' costs are distinct.

A *cut* of an undirected graph $G = (V, E)$ is a partition of its vertex set V into two non-empty sets, A and B.

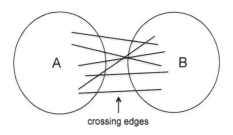

An edge of G *crosses* the cut (A, B) if it has one endpoint in each of A and B.

The Cut Property

Let $G = (V, E)$ be a connected undirected graph with distinct real-valued edge costs. If an edge $e \in E$ is the cheapest edge crossing a cut (A, B), e belongs to every MST of G.[42]

In other words, one way to justify an algorithm's inclusion of an edge e in its solution is to produce a cut of G for which e is the cheapest crossing edge.[43]

(a) Prove the Cut Property.

(b) Use the Cut Property to prove that Prim's algorithm is correct.

(c) Repeat (b) for Kruskal's algorithm.

Problem 15.8 *(H)* Consider a connected undirected graph with distinct real-valued edge costs. A *minimum bottleneck spanning tree (MBST)* is a spanning tree T with the minimum-possible bottleneck (i.e., the minimum maximum edge cost $\max_{e \in T} c_e$).

(a) (Difficult) Give a linear-time algorithm for computing the bottleneck of an MBST.

(b) Does this imply a linear-time algorithm for computing the total cost of an MST?

Programming Problems

Problem 15.9 Implement in your favorite programming language the `Prim` and `Kruskal` algorithms. For bonus points, implement the heap-based version of `Prim` (Section 15.3) and the union-find-based version of `Kruskal` (Section 15.6). Does one of the algorithms seem reliably faster than the other? (See `www.algorithmsilluminated.org` for test cases and challenge data sets.)

---

[42]Readers who have solved Problem 15.6 might want to rephrase the conclusion to "...then e belongs to *the* MST of G."

[43]There's also the *Cycle Property*, which asserts that if an edge e is the costliest on some cycle C, every MST excludes e. You should check that the Cycle Property is equivalent to the converse of Theorem 15.6, which is proved in Problem 15.4.

Chapter 16

Introduction to Dynamic Programming

There's no silver bullet in algorithm design, and the two algorithm design paradigms we've studied so far (divide-and-conquer and greedy algorithms) do not cover all the computational problems you will encounter. The second half of this book will teach you a third design paradigm: the *dynamic programming* paradigm. Dynamic programming is a particularly empowering technique to acquire, as it often leads to efficient solutions beyond the reach of anyone other than serious students of algorithms.

In my experience, most people initially find dynamic programming difficult and counterintuitive. Even more than with other design paradigms, dynamic programming takes practice to perfect. But dynamic programming is relatively formulaic—certainly more so than greedy algorithms—and can be mastered with sufficient practice. This chapter and the next two provide this practice through a half-dozen detailed case studies, including several algorithms belonging to the greatest hits compilation. You'll learn how these famous algorithms work, but even better, you'll add to your programmer toolbox a general and flexible algorithm design technique that you can apply to problems that come up in your own projects. Through these case studies, the power and flexibility of dynamic programming will become clear—it's a technique you simply have to know.

> **Pep Talk**
>
> It is totally normal to feel confused the first time you see dynamic programming. Confusion should not discourage you. It does not represent an intellectual failure on your part, only an opportunity to get even smarter.

16.1 The Weighted Independent Set Problem

I'm not going to tell you what dynamic programming is just yet. Instead, we'll devise from scratch an algorithm for a tricky and concrete computational problem, which will force us to develop a number of new ideas. After we've solved the problem, we'll zoom out and identify the ingredients of our solution that exemplify the general principles of dynamic programming. Then, armed with a template for developing dynamic programming algorithms and an example instantiation, we'll tackle increasingly challenging applications of the paradigm.

16.1.1 Problem Definition

To describe the problem, let $G = (V, E)$ be an undirected graph. An *independent set* of G is a subset $S \subseteq V$ of mutually non-adjacent vertices: for every $v, w \in S$, $(v, w) \notin E$. Equivalently, an independent set does not contain both endpoints of any edge of G. For example, if vertices represent people and edges pairs of people who dislike each other, the independent sets correspond to groups of people who all get along. Or, if the vertices represent classes you're thinking about taking and there is an edge between each pair of conflicting classes, the independent sets correspond to feasible course schedules (assuming you can't be in two places at once).

Quiz 16.1

How many different independent sets does a complete graph with 5 vertices have?

How about a cycle with 5 vertices?

---

a) 1 and 2 (respectively)

b) 5 and 10

c) 6 and 11

d) 6 and 16

(See Section 16.1.4 for the solution and discussion.)

We can now state the *weighted independent set (WIS)* problem:

Problem: Weighted Independent Set (WIS)

Input: An undirected graph $G = (V, E)$ and a nonnegative weight w_v for each vertex $v \in V$.

Output: An independent set $S \subseteq V$ of G with the maximum-possible sum $\sum_{v \in S} w_v$ of vertex weights.

An optimal solution to the WIS problem is called a *maximum-weight independent set (MWIS)*. For example, if vertices represent courses, vertex weights represent units, and edges represent conflicts between courses, the MWIS corresponds to the feasible course schedule with the heaviest load (in units).

The WIS problem is challenging even in the super-simple case of *path graphs*. For example, an input to the problem might look like this (with vertices labeled by their weights):

This graph has 8 independent sets: the empty set, the four singleton sets, the first and third vertices, the first and fourth vertices, and the second and fourth vertices. The last of these has the largest total weight of 8. The number of independent sets of a path graph grows exponentially with the number of vertices (do you see why?), so there is no hope of solving the problem via exhaustive search, except in the tiniest of instances.

16.1.2   The Natural Greedy Algorithm Fails

For many computational problems, greedy algorithms are a great place to start brainstorming. Such algorithms are usually easy to come up with, and even when one fails to solve the problem (as is often the case), the manner in which it fails can help you better understand the intricacies of the problem.

For the WIS problem, perhaps the most natural greedy algorithm is an analog of Kruskal's algorithm: Perform a single pass through the vertices, from best (high-weighted) to worst (lowest-weighted), adding a vertex to the solution-so-far as long as it doesn't conflict with a previously chosen vertex. Given an input graph $G = (V, E)$ with vertex weights, the pseudocode is:

WIS: A Greedy Approach

$S := \emptyset$
sort vertices of V by weight
for each $v \in V$, in nonincreasing order of weight **do**
   if $S \cup \{v\}$ is an independent set of G **then**
      $S := S \cup \{v\}$
return S

Simple enough. But does it work?

Quiz 16.2

What is the total weight of the output of the greedy algorithm when the input graph is the four-vertex path on page 105? Is this the maximum possible?

a) 6; no

b) 6; yes

c) 8; no

d) 8; yes

(See Section 16.1.4 for the solution and discussion.)

Chapters 13–15 spoiled us with a plethora of cherry-picked correct greedy algorithms, but don't forget the warning back on page 3: Greedy algorithms are usually *not* correct.

16.1.3   A Divide-and-Conquer Approach?

The divide-and-conquer algorithm design paradigm (Section 13.1.1) is always worth a shot for problems in which there's a natural way to break the input into smaller subproblems. For the WIS problem with an input path graph $G = (V, E)$, the natural high-level approach is (ignoring the base case):

WIS: A Divide-and-Conquer Approach

$G_1 :=$ first half of G
$G_2 :=$ second half of G
$S_1 :=$ recursively solve the WIS problem on G_1
$S_2 :=$ recursively solve the WIS problem on G_2
combine S_1, S_2 into a solution S for G
return S

The devil is in the details of the combine step. Returning to our running example:

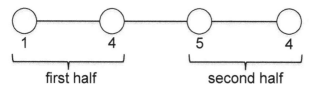

the first and second recursive calls return the second and third vertices as the optimal solutions to their respective subproblems. The union of their solutions is *not* an independent set due to the conflict at the boundary between the two solutions. It's easy to see how to defuse a border conflict when the input graph has only four vertices; when it has hundreds or thousands of vertices, not so much.[1]

Can we do better than a greedy or divide-and-conquer algorithm?

---

[1] The problem can be solved in $O(n^2)$ time by a divide-and-conquer algorithm that makes *four* recursive calls rather than two, where n is the number of vertices. (Do you see how to do this?) Our dynamic programming algorithm for the problem will run in $O(n)$ time.

16.1.4   Solutions to Quizzes 16.1–16.2

Solution to Quiz 16.1

Correct answer: (c). The complete graph has no non-adjacent vertices, so every independent set has at most one vertex. Thus, there are six independent sets: the empty set and the five singleton sets. The cycle has the same six independent sets that the complete graph does, plus some independent sets of size 2. (Every subset of three or more vertices has a pair of adjacent vertices.) It has five size-2 independent sets (as you should verify), for a total of eleven.

Solution to Quiz 16.2

Correct answer: (a). The first iteration of the greedy algorithm commits to the maximum-weight vertex, which is the third vertex (with weight 5). This eliminates the adjacent vertices (the second and fourth ones, both with weight 4) from further consideration. The algorithm is then stuck selecting the first vertex and it outputs an independent set with total weight 6. This is not optimal, as the second and fourth vertices constitute an independent set with total weight 8.

16.2   A Linear-Time Algorithm for WIS in Paths

16.2.1   Optimal Substructure and Recurrence

To quickly solve the WIS problem on path graphs, we'll need to up our game. Key to our approach is the following thought experiment: Suppose someone handed us an optimal solution on a silver platter. What must it look like? Ideally, this thought experiment would show that an optimal solution must be constructed in a prescribed way from optimal solutions to smaller subproblems, thereby narrowing down the field of candidates to a manageable number.[2]

More concretely, let $G = (V, E)$ denote the n-vertex path graph with edges $(v_1, v_2), (v_2, v_3), \ldots, (v_{n-2}, v_{n-1}), (v_{n-1}, v_n)$ and a nonnegative weight w_i for each vertex $v_i \in V$. Assume that $n \geq 2$; otherwise, the answer is obvious. Suppose we magically knew an MWIS $S \subseteq V$

---

[2]There's no circularity in performing a thought experiment about the very object we're trying to compute. As we'll see, such thought experiments can light up a trail that leads directly to an efficient algorithm.

with total weight W. What can we say about it? Here's a tautology: S either contains the final vertex v_n, or it doesn't. Let's examine these cases in reverse order.

Case 1: $v_n \notin S$. Suppose the optimal solution S happens to exclude v_n. Obtain the $(n-1)$-vertex path graph G_{n-1} from G by plucking off the last vertex v_n and the last edge (v_{n-1}, v_n). Because S does not include the last vertex of G, it contains only vertices of G_{n-1} and can be regarded as an independent set of G_{n-1} (still with total weight W)—and not just any old independent set of G_{n-1}, but a *maximum-weight* such set. For if S^* were an independent set of G_{n-1} with total weight $W^* > W$, then S^* would also constitute an independent set of total weight W^* in the larger graph G. This would contradict the supposed optimality of S.

In other words, once you know that an MWIS excludes the last vertex, you know exactly what it looks like: It's an MWIS of the smaller graph G_{n-1}.

Case 2: $v_n \in S$. Suppose S includes the last vertex v_n. As an independent set, S cannot include two consecutive vertices from the path, so it excludes the penultimate vertex: $v_{n-1} \notin S$. Obtain the $(n-2)$-vertex path graph G_{n-2} from G by plucking off the last two vertices and edges:[3]

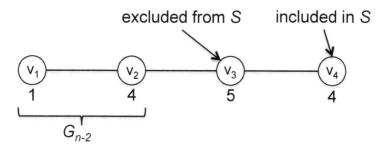

Because S contains v_n and G_{n-2} does not, we can't regard S as an independent set of G_{n-2}. But after removing the last vertex from S, we can: $S - \{v_n\}$ contains neither v_{n-1} nor v_n and hence can be regarded as an independent set of the smaller graph G_{n-2} (with total weight $W - w_n$). Moreover, $S - \{v_n\}$ must be an MWIS

---

[3]When $n = 2$, we interpret G_0 as the empty graph (with no vertices or edges). The only independent set of G_0 is the empty set, which has total weight 0.

of G_{n-2}. For suppose S^* were an independent set of G_{n-2} with total weight $W^* > W - w_n$. Because G_{n-2} (and hence S^*) excludes the penultimate vertex v_{n-1}, blithely adding the last vertex v_n to S^* would not create any conflicts, and so $S^* \cup \{v_n\}$ would be an independent set of G with total weight $W^* + w_n > (W - w_n) + w_n = W$. This would contradict the supposed optimality of S.

In other words, once you know that an MWIS includes the last vertex, you know exactly what it looks like: It's an MWIS of the smaller graph G_{n-2}, supplemented with the final vertex v_n. Summarizing, two and only two candidates are vying to be an MWIS:

Lemma 16.1 (WIS Optimal Substructure) *Let S be an MWIS of a path graph G with at least 2 vertices. Let G_i denote the subgraph of G comprising its first i vertices and $i - 1$ edges. Then, S is either:*

(i) an MWIS of G_{n-1}; or

(ii) an MWIS of G_{n-2}, supplemented with G's final vertex v_n.

Lemma 16.1 singles out the only two possibilities for an MWIS, so whichever option has larger total weight is an optimal solution. We therefore have a recursive formula—a *recurrence*—for the total weight of an MWIS:

Corollary 16.2 (WIS Recurrence) *With the assumptions and notation of Lemma 16.1, let W_i denote the total weight of an MWIS of G_i. (When $i = 0$, interpret W_i as 0.) Then*

$$W_n = \max\{\underbrace{W_{n-1}}_{Case\ 1}, \underbrace{W_{n-2} + w_n}_{Case\ 2}\}.$$

More generally, for every $i = 2, 3, \ldots, n$,

$$W_i = \max\{W_{i-1}, W_{i-2} + w_i\}.$$

The more general statement in Corollary 16.2 follows by invoking the first statement, for each $i = 2, 3, \ldots, n$, with G_i playing the role of the input graph G.

16.2.2   A Naive Recursive Approach

Lemma 16.1 is good news—we've narrowed down the field to just two candidates for the optimal solution! So, why not try both options and return the better of the two? This leads to the following pseudocode, in which the graphs G_{n-1} and G_{n-2} are defined as before:

A Recursive Algorithm for WIS

Input: a path graph G with vertex set $\{v_1, v_2, \ldots, v_n\}$ and a nonnegative weight w_i for each vertex v_i.
Output: a maximum-weight independent set of G.

---

1 **if** $n = 0$ **then**   // base case #1
2   return the empty set
3 **if** $n = 1$ **then**   // base case #2
4   return $\{v_1\}$
    // recursion when $n \geq 2$
5 $S_1 :=$ recursively compute an MWIS of G_{n-1}
6 $S_2 :=$ recursively compute an MWIS of G_{n-2}
7 return S_1 or $S_2 \cup \{v_n\}$, whichever has higher weight

---

A straightforward proof by induction shows that this algorithm is guaranteed to compute a maximum-weight independent set.[4] What about the running time?

Quiz 16.3

What is the asymptotic running time of the recursive WIS algorithm, as a function of the number n of vertices? (Choose the strongest correct statement.)

a) $O(n)$

b) $O(n \log n)$

---

[4]The proof proceeds by induction on the number n of vertices. The base cases ($n = 0, 1$) are clearly correct. For the inductive step ($n \geq 2$), the inductive hypothesis guarantees that S_1 and S_2 are indeed MWISs of G_{n-1} and G_{n-2}, respectively. Lemma 16.1 implies that the better of S_1 and $S_2 \cup \{v_n\}$ is an MWIS of G, and this is the output of the algorithm.

c) $O(n^2)$

d) none of the above

(See Section 16.2.5 for the solution and discussion.)

16.2.3   Recursion with a Cache

Quiz 16.3 shows that our recursive WIS algorithm is no better than exhaustive search. The next quiz contains the key to unlocking a radical running time improvement. Think about it carefully before reading the solution.

Quiz 16.4

Each of the (exponentially many) recursive calls of the recursive WIS algorithm is responsible for computing an MWIS of a specified input graph. Ranging over all of the calls, how many *distinct* input graphs are ever considered?

a) $\Theta(1)^5$

b) $\Theta(n)$

c) $\Theta(n^2)$

d) $2^{\Theta(n)}$

(See Section 16.2.5 for the solution and discussion.)

Quiz 16.4 implies that the exponential running time of our recursive WIS algorithm stems solely from its absurd redundancy, solving the same subproblems from scratch over, and over, and over, and over again. Here's an idea: The first time we solve a subproblem, why not save the result in a cache once and for all? Then, if we encounter the

---

[5]If big-O notation is analogous to "less than or equal," then big-theta notion is analogous to "equal." Formally, a function $f(n)$ is $\Theta(g(n))$ if there are constants c_1 and c_2 such that $f(n)$ is wedged between $c_1 \cdot g(n)$ and $c_2 \cdot g(n)$ for all sufficiently large n.

same subproblem later, we can look up its solution in the cache in constant time.[6]

Blending caching into the pseudocode on page 111 is easy. The results of past computations are stored in a globally visible length-$(n+1)$ array A, with $A[i]$ storing an MWIS of G_i, where G_i comprises the first i vertices and the first $i-1$ edges of the original input graph (and G_0 is the empty graph). In line 6, the algorithm now first checks whether the array A already contains the relevant solution S_1; if not, it computes S_1 recursively as before and caches the result in A. Similarly, the new version of line 7 either looks up or recursively computes and caches S_2, as needed.

Each of the $n+1$ subproblems is now solved from scratch only once. Caching surely speeds up the algorithm, but by how much? Properly implemented, the running time drops from exponential to *linear*. This dramatic speedup will be easier to see after we reformulate our top-down recursive algorithm as a bottom-up iterative one—and the latter is usually what you want to implement in practice, anyway.

16.2.4   An Iterative Bottom-Up Implementation

As part of figuring out how to incorporate caching into our recursive WIS algorithm, we realized that there are exactly $n+1$ relevant subproblems, corresponding to all possible prefixes of the input graph (Quiz 16.4).

WIS in Path Graphs: Subproblems

Compute W_i, the total weight of an MWIS of the prefix graph G_i.

(For each $i = 0, 1, 2, \ldots, n$.)

For now, we focus on computing the total weight of an MWIS for a subproblem. Section 16.3 shows how to also identify the vertices of an MWIS.

Now that we know which subproblems are the important ones, why not cut to the chase and systematically solve them one by one?

---

[6]This technique of caching the result of a computation to avoid redoing it later is sometimes called *memoization*.

The solution to a subproblem depends on the solutions to two smaller subproblems. To ensure that these two solutions are readily available, it makes sense to work bottom-up, starting with the base cases and building up to ever-larger subproblems.

WIS

Input: a path graph G with vertex set $\{v_1, v_2, \ldots, v_n\}$ and a nonnegative weight w_i for each vertex v_i.
Output: the total weight of a maximum-weight independent set of G.

$A := $ length-$(n+1)$ array   // subproblem solutions
$A[0] := 0$ // base case #1
$A[1] := w_1$ // base case #2
for $i = 2$ to n **do**
   // use recurrence from Corollary 16.2
   $A[i] := \max\{\underbrace{A[i-1]}_{\text{Case 1}}, \underbrace{A[i-2] + w_i}_{\text{Case 2}}\}$
return $A[n]$ // solution to largest subproblem

The length-$(n+1)$ array A is indexed from 0 to n. By the time an iteration of the main loop must compute the subproblem solution $A[i]$, the values $A[i-1]$ and $A[i-2]$ of the two relevant smaller subproblems have already been computed in previous iterations (or in the base cases). Thus, each loop iteration takes $O(1)$ time, for a blazingly fast running time of $O(n)$.

For example, for the input graph

you should check that the final array values are:

prefix length i

0	1	2	3	4	5	6
0	3	3	4	9	9	14

At the conclusion of the WIS algorithm, each array entry $A[i]$ stores the total weight of an MWIS of the graph G_i that comprises the first i vertices and $i - 1$ edges of the input graph. This follows from an inductive argument similar to the one in footnote 4. The base cases $A[0]$ and $A[1]$ are clearly correct. When computing $A[i]$ with $i \geq 2$, by induction, the values $A[i - 1]$ and $A[i - 2]$ are indeed the total weights of MWISs of G_{i-1} and G_{i-2}, respectively. Corollary 16.2 then implies that $A[i]$ is computed correctly, as well. In the example above, the total weight of an MWIS in the original input graph is the value in the final array entry (14), corresponding to the independent set consisting of the first, fourth, and sixth vertices.

Theorem 16.3 (Properties of WIS) *For every path graph and non-negative vertex weights, the WIS algorithm runs in linear time and returns the total weight of a maximum-weight independent set.*

16.2.5   Solutions to Quizzes 16.3–16.4

Solution to Quiz 16.3

Correct answer: (d). Superficially, the recursion pattern looks similar to that of $O(n \log n)$-time divide-and-conquer algorithms like MergeSort, with two recursive calls followed by an easy combine step. But there's a big difference: The MergeSort algorithm throws away half the input before recursing, while our recursive WIS algorithm throws away only one or two vertices (perhaps out of thousands or millions). Both algorithms have recursion trees with branching factor 2.[7] The former has roughly $\log_2 n$ levels and, hence, only a linear number of leaves. The latter has no leaves until levels $n/2$ and later, which implies that it has at least $2^{n/2}$ leaves. We conclude that the running time of the recursive algorithm grows exponentially with n.

Solution to Quiz 16.4

Correct answer: (b). How does the input graph change upon passage to a recursive call? Either one or two vertices and edges are

---

[7]Every recursive algorithm can be associated with a recursion tree, in which the nodes of the tree correspond to all the algorithm's recursive calls. The root of the tree corresponds to the initial call to the algorithm (with the original input), with one child at the next level for each of its recursive calls. The leaves at the bottom of the tree correspond to the recursive calls that trigger a base case and make no further recursive calls.

plucked off the end of the graph. Thus, an invariant throughout the recursion is that every recursive call is given some *prefix* G_i as its input graph, where G_i denotes the first i vertices and $i - 1$ edges of the original input graph (and G_0 denotes the empty graph):

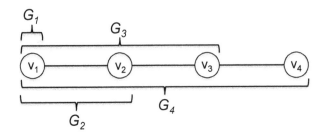

There are only $n + 1$ such graphs $(G_0, G_1, G_2, \ldots, G_n)$, where n is the number of vertices in the input graph. Therefore, only $n + 1$ distinct subproblems ever get solved across the exponential number of different recursive calls.

16.3   A Reconstruction Algorithm

The WIS algorithm in Section 16.2.4 computes only the *weight* possessed by an MWIS of a path graph, not an MWIS itself. A simple hack is to modify the WIS algorithm so that each array entry $A[i]$ records both the total weight of an MWIS of the ith subproblem G_i *and* the vertices of an MWIS of G_i that realizes this value.

A better approach, which saves both time and space, is to use a postprocessing step to reconstruct an MWIS from the tracks in the mud left by the WIS algorithm in its subproblem array A. For starters, how do we know whether the last vertex v_n of the input graph G belongs to an MWIS? The key is again Lemma 16.1, which states that two and only two candidates are vying to be an MWIS of G: an MWIS of the graph G_{n-1}, and an MWIS of the graph G_{n-2}, supplemented with v_n. Which one is it? The one with larger total weight. How do we know which one that is? Just look at the clues left in the array A! The final values of $A[n-1]$ and $A[n-2]$ record the total weights of MWISs of G_{n-1} and G_{n-2}, respectively. So:

1. If $A[n-1] \geq A[n-2] + w_n$, an MWIS of G_{n-1} is also an MWIS of G_n.

2. If $A[n-2] + w_n \geq A[n-1]$, supplementing an MWIS of G_{n-2} with v_n yields an MWIS of G_n.

In the first case, we know to exclude v_n from our solution and can continue the reconstruction process from v_{n-1}. In the second case, we know to include v_n in our solution, which forces us to exclude v_{n-1}. The reconstruction process then resumes from v_{n-2}.[8]

WIS Reconstruction

Input: the array A computed by the WIS algorithm for a path graph G with vertex set $\{v_1, v_2, \ldots, v_n\}$ and a nonnegative weight w_i for each vertex v_i.
Output: a maximum-weight independent set of G.

$S := \emptyset$ // vertices in an MWIS
$i := n$
while $i \geq 2$ **do**
    if $A[i-1] \geq A[i-2] + w_i$ **then**   // Case 1 wins
        $i := i - 1$ // exclude v_i
    else   // Case 2 wins
        $S := S \cup \{v_i\}$ // include v_i
        $i := i - 2$ // exclude v_{i-1}
if $i = 1$ **then**   // base case #2
    $S := S \cup \{v_1\}$
return S

WIS Reconstruction does a single backward pass over the array A and spends $O(1)$ time per loop iteration, so it runs in $O(n)$ time. The inductive proof of correctness is similar to that for the WIS algorithm (Theorem 16.3).[9]

For example, for the input graph

---

[8]If there is a tie ($A[n-2] + w_n = A[n-1]$), both options lead to an optimal solution.

[9]The keen reader might complain that it's wasteful to recompute comparisons of the form $A[i-1]$ vs. $A[i-2] + w_i$, which have already been made by the WIS algorithm. If that algorithm is modified to cache the comparison results (in effect, remembering which case of the recurrence was used to fill in each array entry), these results can be looked up rather than recomputed in the WIS Reconstruction algorithm. This idea will be particularly important for some of the harder problems studied in Chapters 17 and 18.

the WIS Reconstruction algorithm includes v_6 (forcing v_5's exclusion), includes v_4 (forcing v_3's exclusion), excludes v_2, and includes v_1:

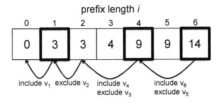

16.4 The Principles of Dynamic Programming

16.4.1 A Three-Step Recipe

Guess what? With WIS, we just designed our first dynamic programming algorithm! The general dynamic programming paradigm can be summarized by a three-step recipe. It is best understood through examples; we have only one so far, so I encourage you to revisit this section after we finish a few more case studies.

The Dynamic Programming Paradigm

1. Identify a relatively small collection of subproblems.

2. Show how to quickly and correctly solve "larger" subproblems given the solutions to "smaller" ones.

3. Show how to quickly and correctly infer the final solution from the solutions to all of the subproblems.

After these three steps are implemented, the corresponding dynamic programming algorithm writes itself: Systematically solve all the subproblems one by one, working from "smallest" to "largest," and extract the final solution from those of the subproblems.

In our solution to the WIS problem in n-vertex path graphs, we implemented the first step by identifying a collection of $n + 1$ subproblems. For $i = 0, 1, 2, \ldots, n$, the ith subproblem is to compute the total weight of an MWIS of the graph G_i consisting of the first i

vertices and $i - 1$ edges of the input graph (where G_0 denotes the empty graph). There is an obvious way to order the subproblems from "smallest" to "largest," namely $G_0, G_1, G_2, \ldots, G_n$. The recurrence in Corollary 16.2 is a formula that implements the second step by showing how to compute the solution to the ith subproblem in $O(1)$ time from the solutions to the $(i - 2)$th and $(i - 1)$th subproblems. The third step is easy: Return the solution to the largest subproblem, which is the same as the original problem.

16.4.2   Desirable Subproblem Properties

The key that unlocks the potential of dynamic programming for solving a problem is the identification of the right collection of subproblems. What properties do we want them to satisfy? Assuming we perform at least a constant amount of work solving each subproblem, the number of subproblems is a lower bound on the running time of our algorithm. Thus, we'd like the number of subproblems to be as low as possible—our WIS solution used only a linear number of subproblems, which is usually the best-case scenario. Similarly, the time required to solve a subproblem (given solutions to smaller subproblems) and to infer the final solution will factor into the algorithm's overall running time.

For example, suppose an algorithm solves at most $f(n)$ different subproblems (working systematically from "smallest" to "largest"), using at most $g(n)$ time for each, and performs at most $h(n)$ postprocessing work to extract the final solution (where n denotes the input size). The algorithm's running time is then at most

$$\underbrace{f(n)}_{\text{\# subproblems}} \times \underbrace{g(n)}_{\substack{\text{time per subproblem} \\ \text{(given previous solutions)}}} + \underbrace{h(n)}_{\text{postprocessing}} . \qquad (16.1)$$

The three steps of the recipe call for keeping $f(n)$, $g(n)$, and $h(n)$, respectively, as small as possible. In the basic WIS algorithm, without the WIS Reconstruction postprocessing step, we have $f(n) = O(n)$, $g(n) = O(1)$, and $h(n) = O(1)$, for an overall running time of $O(n)$. If we include the reconstruction step, the $h(n)$ term jumps to $O(n)$, but the overall running time $O(n) \times O(1) + O(n) = O(n)$ remains linear.

16.4.3   A Repeatable Thought Process

When devising your own dynamic programming algorithms, the heart of the matter is figuring out the magical collection of subproblems. After that, everything else falls into place in a fairly formulaic way. But how would you ever come up with them? If you have a black belt in dynamic programming, you might be able to just stare at a problem and intuitively know what the subproblems should be. White belts, however, still have a lot of training to do. In our case studies, rather than plucking subproblems from the sky, we'll carry out a thought process that naturally leads to a collection of subproblems (as we did for the WIS problem). This process is repeatable and you can mimic it when you apply the dynamic programming paradigm to problems that arise in your own projects.

The main idea is to reason about the structure of an optimal solution, identifying the different ways it might be constructed from optimal solutions to smaller subproblems. This thought experiment can lead to both the identification of the relevant subproblems and a recurrence (analogous to Corollary 16.2) that expresses the solution of a subproblem as a function of the solutions of smaller subproblems. A dynamic programming algorithm can then fill in an array with subproblem solutions, proceeding from smaller to larger subproblems and using the recurrence to compute each array entry.

16.4.4   Dynamic Programming vs. Divide-and-Conquer

Readers familiar with the divide-and-conquer algorithm design paradigm (Section 13.1.1) might recognize some similarities to dynamic programming, especially the latter's top-down recursive formulation (Sections 16.2.2–16.2.3). Both paradigms recursively solve smaller subproblems and combine the results into a solution to the original problem. Here are six differences between typical uses of the two paradigms:

1. Each recursive call of a typical divide-and-conquer algorithm commits to a single way of dividing the input into smaller subproblems.[10] Each recursive call of a dynamic programming

---

[10]For example, in the MergeSort algorithm, every recursive call divides its input array into its left and right halves. The QuickSort algorithm invokes a

algorithm keeps its options open, considering multiple ways of defining smaller subproblems and choosing the best of them.[11]

2. Because each recursive call of a dynamic programming algorithm tries out multiple choices of smaller subproblems, subproblems generally recur across different recursive calls; caching subproblem solutions is then a no-brainer optimization. In most divide-and-conquer algorithms, all the subproblems are distinct and there's no point in caching their solutions.[12]

3. Most of the canonical applications of the divide-and-conquer paradigm replace a straightforward polynomial-time algorithm for a task with a faster divide-and-conquer version.[13] The killer applications of dynamic programming are polynomial-time algorithms for optimization problems for which straightforward solutions (like exhaustive search) require an exponential amount of time.

4. In a divide-and-conquer algorithm, subproblems are chosen primarily to optimize the running time; correctness often takes care of itself.[14] In dynamic programming, subproblems are usually chosen with correctness in mind, come what may with the running time.[15]

5. Relatedly, a divide-and-conquer algorithm generally recurses on subproblems with size at most a constant fraction (like 50%) of the input. Dynamic programming has no qualms about

---

partitioning subroutine to choose how to split the input array in two, and then commits to this division for the remainder of its execution.

[11]For example, in the WIS algorithm, each recursive call chooses between a subproblem with one fewer vertex and one with two fewer vertices.

[12]For example, in the MergeSort and QuickSort algorithms, every subproblem corresponds to a different subarray of the input array.

[13]For example, the MergeSort algorithm brings the running time of sorting a length-n array down from the straightforward bound of $O(n^2)$ to $O(n \log n)$. Other examples include Karatsuba's algorithm (which improves the running time of multiplying two n-digit numbers from $O(n^2)$ to $O(n^{1.59})$) and Strassen's algorithm (for multiplying two $n \times n$ matrices in $O(n^{2.81})$ rather than $O(n^3)$ time).

[14]For example, the QuickSort algorithm always correctly sorts the input array, no matter how good or bad its chosen pivot elements are.

[15]Our dynamic programming algorithm for the knapsack problem in Section 16.5 is a good example.

recursing on subproblems that are barely smaller than the input (like in the WIS algorithm), if necessary for correctness.

6. The divide-and-conquer paradigm can be viewed as a special case of dynamic programming, in which each recursive call chooses a fixed collection of subproblems to solve recursively. As the more sophisticated paradigm, dynamic programming applies to a wider range of problems than divide-and-conquer, but it is also more technically demanding to apply (at least until you've had sufficient practice).

Confronted with a new problem, which paradigm should you use? If you see a divide-and-conquer solution, by all means use it. If all your divide-and-conquer attempts fail—and especially if they fail because the combine step always seems to require redoing a lot of computation from scratch—it's time to try dynamic programming.

16.4.5   Why "Dynamic Programming?"

You might be wondering where the weird moniker "dynamic programming" came from; the answer is no clearer now that we know how the paradigm works than it was before.

The first point of confusion is the anachronistic use of the word "programming." In modern times it refers to coding, but back in the 1950s "programming" usually meant "planning." (For example, it has this meaning in the phrase "television programming.") What about "dynamic?" For the full story, I refer you to the father of dynamic programming himself, Richard E. Bellman, writing about his time working at the RAND Corporation:

> The 1950's were not good years for mathematical research. We had a very interesting gentleman in Washington named Wilson. He was Secretary of Defense, and he actually had a pathological fear and hatred of the word, research. I'm not using the term lightly; I'm using it precisely. His face with suffuse, he would turn red, and he would get violent if people used the term, research, in his presence. You can imagine how he felt, then, about the term, mathematical. The RAND Corporation was employed by the Air Force, and the Air Force had Wilson as its boss, essentially.

Hence, I felt I had to do something to shield Wilson and the Air Force from the fact that I was really doing mathematics inside the RAND Corporation. What title, what name, could I choose? In the first place I was interested in planning, in decision making, in thinking. But planning, is not a good word for various reasons. I decided therefore to use the word, "programming." ... ["Dynamic"] has a very interesting property as an adjective, and that is it's impossible to use the word, dynamic, in the pejorative sense. Try thinking of some combination that will possibly give it a pejorative meaning. It's impossible. Thus, I thought dynamic programming was a good name. It was something not even a Congressman could object to. So I used it as an umbrella for my activities.[16]

16.5   The Knapsack Problem

Our second case study concerns the well-known *knapsack problem*. Following the same thought process we used to develop the WIS algorithm in Section 16.2, we'll arrive at the famous dynamic programming solution to the problem.

16.5.1   Problem Definition

An instance of the knapsack problem is specified by $2n + 1$ positive integers, where n is the number of "items" (which are labeled arbitrarily from 1 to n): a value v_i and a size s_i for each item i, and a knapsack capacity C.[17] The responsibility of an algorithm is to select a subset of the items. The total value of the items should be as large as possible while still fitting in the knapsack, meaning their total size should be at most C.

[16]Richard E. Bellman, *Eye of the Hurricane: An Autobiography*, World Scientific, 1984, page 159.

[17]It's actually not important that the item values are integers (as opposed to arbitrary positive real numbers). It *is* important that the item sizes are integers, as we'll see in due time.

Problem: Knapsack

Input: Item values $v_1, v_2, \ldots, v_n$, item sizes $s_1, s_2, \ldots, s_n$, and a knapsack capacity C. (All positive integers.)

Output: A subset $S \subseteq \{1, 2, \ldots, n\}$ of items with the maximum-possible sum $\sum_{i \in S} v_i$ of values, subject to having total size $\sum_{i \in S} s_i$ at most C.

Quiz 16.5

Consider an instance of the knapsack problem with knapsack capacity $C = 6$ and four items:

Item	Value	Size
1	3	4
2	2	3
3	4	2
4	4	3

What is the total value of an optimal solution?

a) 6

b) 7

c) 8

d) 10

(See Section 16.5.7 for the solution and discussion.)

I could tell you a cheesy story about a knapsack-wielding burglar who breaks into a house and wants to make off quickly with the best pile of loot possible, but this would do a disservice to the problem, which is actually quite fundamental. Whenever you have a scarce resource that you want to use in the smartest way possible, you're talking about a knapsack problem. On which goods and services should you spend your paycheck to get the most value? Given an operating budget and a set of job candidates with differing productivities and requested salaries, whom should you hire? These are examples of knapsack problems.

16.5.2   Optimal Substructure and Recurrence

To apply the dynamic programming paradigm to the knapsack problem, we must figure out the right collection of subproblems. As with the WIS problem, we'll arrive at them by reasoning about the structure of optimal solutions and identifying the different ways they can be constructed from optimal solutions to smaller subproblems. Another deliverable of this exercise will be a recurrence for quickly computing the solution to a subproblem from those of two smaller subproblems.

Consider an instance of the knapsack problem with item values $v_1, v_2, \ldots, v_n$, item sizes $s_1, s_2, \ldots, s_n$, and knapsack capacity C, and suppose someone handed us on a silver platter an optimal solution $S \subseteq \{1, 2, \ldots, n\}$ with total value $V = \sum_{i \in S} v_i$. What must it look like? As with the WIS problem, we start with a tautology: S either contains the last item (item n) or it doesn't.[18]

Case 1: $n \notin S$. Because the optimal solution S excludes the last item, it can be regarded as a feasible solution (still with total value V and total size at most C) to the smaller problem consisting of only the first $n - 1$ items (and knapsack capacity C). Moreover, S must be an optimal solution to the smaller subproblem: If there were a solution $S^* \subseteq \{1, 2, \ldots, n - 1\}$ with total size at most C and total value greater than V, it would also constitute such a solution in the original instance. This would contradict the supposed optimality of S.

Case 2: $n \in S$. The trickier case is when the optimal solution S makes use of the last item n. This case can occur only when $s_n \leq C$. We can't regard S as a feasible solution to a smaller problem with only the first $n - 1$ items, but we can after removing item n. Is $S - \{n\}$ an optimal solution to a smaller subproblem?

---

[18]The WIS problem on path graphs is inherently sequential, with the vertices ordered along the path. This naturally led to subproblems that correspond to prefixes of the input. The items in the knapsack problem are not inherently ordered, but to identify the right collection of subproblems, it's helpful to mimic our previous approach and *pretend* they're ordered in some arbitrary way. A "prefix" of the items then corresponds to the first i items in our arbitrary ordering (for some $i \in \{0, 1, 2, \ldots, n\}$). Many other dynamic programming algorithms use this same trick.

Quiz 16.6

Which of the following statements hold for the set $S - \{n\}$? (Choose all that apply.)

a) It is an optimal solution to the subproblem consisting of the first $n - 1$ items and knapsack capacity C.

b) It is an optimal solution to the subproblem consisting of the first $n - 1$ items and knapsack capacity $C - v_n$.

c) It is an optimal solution to the subproblem consisting of the first $n - 1$ items and knapsack capacity $C - s_n$.

d) It might not be feasible if the knapsack capacity is only $C - s_n$.

(See Section 16.5.7 for the solution and discussion.)

This case analysis shows that two and only two candidates are vying to be an optimal knapsack solution:

Lemma 16.4 (Knapsack Optimal Substructure) *Let S be an optimal solution to a knapsack problem with $n \geq 1$ items, item values $v_1, v_2, \ldots, v_n$, item sizes $s_1, s_2, \ldots, s_n$, and knapsack capacity C. Then, S is either:*

(i) an optimal solution for the first $n - 1$ items with knapsack capacity C; or

(ii) an optimal solution for the first $n - 1$ items with knapsack capacity $C - s_n$, supplemented with the last item n.

The solution in (i) is always an option for the optimal solution. The solution in (ii) is an option if and only if $s_n \leq C$; in this case, s_n units of capacity are effectively reserved in advance for item n.[19] The option with the larger total value is an optimal solution, leading to the following recurrence:

---

[19]This is analogous to, in the WIS problem on path graphs, excluding the penultimate vertex of the graph to reserve space for the final vertex.

Corollary 16.5 (Knapsack Recurrence) *With the assumptions and notation of Lemma 16.4, let $V_{i,c}$ denote the maximum total value of a subset of the first i items with total size at most c. (When $i = 0$, interpret $V_{i,c}$ as 0.) For every $i = 1, 2, \ldots, n$ and $c = 0, 1, 2, \ldots, C$,*

$$
V_{i,c} = \begin{cases} \underbrace{V_{i-1,c}}_{Case\ 1} & \text{if } s_i > c \\[2em] \max\{\underbrace{V_{i-1,c}}_{Case\ 1}, \underbrace{V_{i-1,c-s_i} + v_i}_{Case\ 2}\} & \text{if } s_i \leq c. \end{cases}
$$

Because both c and items' sizes are integers, the residual capacity $c - s_i$ in the second case is also an integer.

16.5.3   The Subproblems

The next step is to define the collection of relevant subproblems and solve them systematically using the recurrence identified in Corollary 16.5. For now, we focus on computing the total value of an optimal solution for each subproblem. As in the WIS problem on path graphs, we'll be able to reconstruct the items in an optimal solution to the original problem from this information.

Back in the WIS problem on path graphs, we used only one parameter i to index subproblems, where i was the length of the prefix of the input graph. For the knapsack problem, we can see from Lemma 16.4 and Corollary 16.5 that subproblems should be parameterized by *two* indices: the length i of the prefix of available items and the available knapsack capacity c.[20] Ranging over all relevant values of the two parameters, we obtain our subproblems:

Knapsack: Subproblems

Compute $V_{i,c}$, the total value of an optimal knapsack solution with the first i items and knapsack capacity c.

(For each $i = 0, 1, 2, \ldots, n$ and $c = 0, 1, 2, \ldots, C$.)

---

[20]In the WIS problem on path graphs, there's only one dimension in which a subproblem can get smaller (by having fewer vertices). In the knapsack problem, there are two (by having fewer items, or less knapsack capacity).

The largest subproblem (with $i = n$ and $c = C$) is exactly the same as the original problem. Because all item sizes and the knapsack capacity C are positive integers, and because capacity is always reduced by the size of some item (to reserve space for it), the only residual capacities that can ever come up are the integers between 0 and C.[21]

16.5.4   A Dynamic Programming Algorithm

Given the subproblems and recurrence, a dynamic programming algorithm for the knapsack problem practically writes itself.

Knapsack

Input: item values $v_1, \ldots, v_n$, item sizes $s_1, \ldots, s_n$, and a knapsack capacity C (all positive integers).
Output: the maximum total value of a subset $S \subseteq \{1, 2, \ldots, n\}$ with $\sum_{i \in S} s_i \leq C$.

```
// subproblem solutions (indexed from 0)
```
$A := (n+1) \times (C+1)$ two-dimensional array
```
// base case (i = 0)
for c = 0 to C do
```
    $A[0][c] = 0$
```
// systematically solve all subproblems
for i = 1 to n do
    for c = 0 to C do
        // use recurrence from Corollary 16.5
        if s_i > c then
```
            $A[i][c] := A[i-1][c]$
```
        else
```
            $A[i][c] :=$
            $\max\{\underbrace{A[i-1][c]}_{\text{Case 1}}, \underbrace{A[i-1][c-s_i] + v_i}_{\text{Case 2}}\}$
```
return A[n][C] // solution to largest subproblem
```

---

[21] Or, thinking recursively, each recursive call removes the last item and an integer number of units of capacity. The only subproblems that can arise in this way involve some prefix of the items and some integer residual capacity.

The array A is now two-dimensional to reflect the two indices i and c used to parameterize the subproblems. By the time an iteration of the double for loop must compute the subproblem solution $A[i][c]$, the values $A[i-1][c]$ and $A[i-1][c-s_i]$ of the two relevant smaller subproblems have already been computed in the previous iteration of the outer loop (or in the base case). We conclude that the algorithm spends $O(1)$ time solving each of the $(n+1)(C+1) = O(nC)$ subproblems, for an overall running time of $O(nC)$.[22,23]

Finally, as with WIS, the correctness of Knapsack follows by induction on the number of items, with the recurrence in Corollary 16.5 used to justify the inductive step.

Theorem 16.6 (Properties of Knapsack) *For every instance of the knapsack problem, the **Knapsack** algorithm returns the total value of an optimal solution and runs in $O(nC)$ time, where n is the number of items and C is the knapsack capacity.*

16.5.5   Example

Recall the four-item example from Quiz 16.5, with $C = 6$:

Item	Value	Size
1	3	4
2	2	3
3	4	2
4	4	3

Because $n = 4$ and $C = 6$, the array A in the Knapsack algorithm can be visualized as a table with 5 columns (corresponding to $i = 0, 1, \ldots, 4$) and 7 rows (corresponding to $c = 0, 1, \ldots, 6$). The final array values are:

---

[22]In the notation of (16.1), $f(n) = O(nC)$, $g(n) = O(1)$, and $h(n) = O(1)$.

[23]The running time bound of $O(nC)$ is impressive only if C is small, for example, if $C = O(n)$ or ideally even smaller. In *Part 4* we'll see the reason for the not-so-blazingly fast running time—there is a precise sense in which the knapsack problem is a difficult problem.

residual capacity c					
6	0	3	3	7	8
5	0	3	3	6	8
4	0	3	3	4	4
3	0	0	2	4	4
2	0	0	0	4	4
1	0	0	0	0	0
0	0	0	0	0	0
	0	1	2	3	4

prefix length i

Knapsack computes these entries column by column (working left to
right), and within a column from bottom to top. To fill in an entry
of the ith column, the algorithm compares the entry immediately to
the left (corresponding to case 1) to v_i plus the entry one column to
the left and s_i rows down (case 2). For example, for $A[2][5]$ the better
option is to skip the second item and inherit the "3" immediately to
the left, while for $A[3][5]$ the better option is to include the third item
and achieve 4 (for v_3) plus the 2 in the entry $A[2][3]$.

16.5.6   Reconstruction

The Knapsack algorithm computes only the total value of an optimal
solution, not the optimal solution itself. As with the WIS algorithm,
we can reconstruct an optimal solution by tracing back through the
filled-in array A. Starting from the largest subproblem in the upper-
right corner, the reconstruction algorithm checks which case of the
recurrence was used to compute $A[n][C]$. If it was case 1, the algorithm
omits item n and resumes reconstruction from the entry $A[n-1][C]$.
If it was case 2, the algorithm includes item n in its solution and
resumes reconstruction from the entry $A[n-1][C-s_n]$.

Knapsack Reconstruction

Input: the array A computed by the Knapsack
algorithm with item values $v_1, v_2, \ldots, v_n$, item sizes
$s_1, s_2, \ldots, s_n$, and knapsack capacity C.
Output: an optimal knapsack solution.

$S := \emptyset$ `// items in an optimal solution`
$c := C$ `// remaining capacity`
for $i = n$ downto 1 **do**
    if $s_i \leq c$ and $A[i-1][c-s_i] + v_i \geq A[i-1][c]$ **then**
        $S := S \cup \{i\}$ `// Case 2 wins, include` i
        $c := c - s_i$ `// reserve space for it`
    `// else skip` i`, capacity stays the same`
return S

The Knapsack Reconstruction postprocessing step runs in $O(n)$
time (with $O(1)$ work per iteration of the main loop), which is much
faster than the $O(nC)$ time used to fill in the array in the Knapsack
algorithm.[24]

For instance, tracing back through the array from the example on
page 130 yields the optimal solution $\{3, 4\}$:

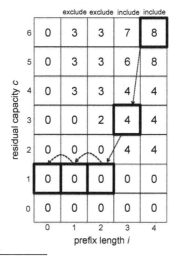

---

[24]In the notation of (16.1), postprocessing with the Knapsack Reconstruction
algorithm increases the $h(n)$ term to $O(n)$. The overall running time $O(nC) \times$
$O(1) + O(n) = O(nC)$ remains the same.

16.5.7   Solutions to Quizzes 16.5–16.6

Solution to Quiz 16.5

Correct answer: (c). Because the knapsack capacity is 6, there is
no room to choose more than two items. The most valuable pair of
items is the third and fourth ones (with total value 8), and these fit
in the knapsack (with total size 5).

Solution to Quiz 16.6

Correct answer: (c). The most obviously false statement is (b),
which doesn't even typecheck (C is in units of size, v_n in units of
value). For example, v_n could be bigger than C, in which case $C - v_n$
is negative and meaningless. For (d), because S is feasible for the
original problem, its total size is at most C; after n is removed from S,
the total size drops to at most $C - s_n$ and, hence, $S - \{n\}$ is feasible
for the reduced capacity. Answer (a) is a natural guess but is also
incorrect.[25]

In (c), we are effectively reserving s_n units of capacity for item n's
inclusion, which leaves a residual capacity of $C - s_n$. $S - \{n\}$ is a
feasible solution to the smaller subproblem (with knapsack capacity $C - s_n$) with total value $V - v_n$. If there were a better solution
$S^* \subseteq \{1, 2, \ldots, n-1\}$, with total value $V^* > V - v_n$ and total size
at most $C - s_n$, then $S^* \cup \{n\}$ would have total size at most C and
total value $V^* + v_n > (V - v_n) + v_n = V$. This would contradict the
supposed optimality of S for the original problem.

The Upshot

★ Dynamic programming follows a three-step
recipe: (i) identify a relatively small collection of subproblems; (ii) show how to quickly
solve "larger" subproblems given the solutions
to "smaller" ones; and (iii) show how to quickly
infer the final solution from the solutions to all

---

[25]For example, suppose $C = 2$ and consider two items, with $v_1 = s_1 = 1$ and
$v_2 = s_2 = 2$. The optimal solution S is $\{2\}$. $S - \{2\}$ is the empty set, but the
only optimal solution to the subproblem consisting of the first item and knapsack
capacity 2 is $\{1\}$.

the subproblems.

☆ A dynamic programming algorithm that solves at most $f(n)$ different subproblems, using at most $g(n)$ time for each, and performs at most $h(n)$ postprocessing work to extract the final solution runs in $O(f(n) \cdot g(n) + h(n))$ time, where n denotes the input size.

☆ The right collection of subproblems and a recurrence for systematically solving them can be identified by reasoning about the structure of an optimal solution and the different ways it might be constructed from optimal solutions to smaller subproblems.

☆ Typical dynamic programming algorithms fill in an array with the values of subproblems' solutions, and then trace back through the filled-in array to reconstruct the solution itself.

☆ An independent set of an undirected graph is a subset of mutually non-adjacent vertices.

☆ In n-vertex path graphs, a maximum-weight independent set can be computed using dynamic programming in $O(n)$ time.

☆ In the knapsack problem, given n items with values and sizes and a knapsack capacity C (all positive integers), the goal is to select the maximum-value subset of items with total size at most C.

☆ The knapsack problem can be solved using dynamic programming in $O(nC)$ time.

Test Your Understanding

Problem 16.1 *(S)* Consider the input graph

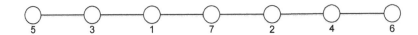

where vertices are labeled with their weights. What are the final array entries of the WIS algorithm from Section 16.2, and which vertices belong to the MWIS?

Problem 16.2 *(H)* Which of the following statements hold? (Choose all that apply.)

a) The WIS and WIS Reconstruction algorithms of Sections 16.2 and 16.3 always return a solution that includes a maximum-weight vertex.

b) When vertices' weights are distinct, the WIS and WIS Reconstruction algorithms never return a solution that includes a minimum-weight vertex.

c) If a vertex v does not belong to an MWIS of the prefix G_i comprising the first i vertices and $i-1$ edges of the input graph, it does not belong to any MWIS of $G_{i+1}, G_{i+2}, \ldots, G_n$ either.

d) If a vertex v does not belong to an MWIS of G_{i-1} or G_i, it does not belong to any MWIS of $G_{i+1}, G_{i+2}, \ldots, G_n$ either.

Problem 16.3 *(H)* This problem outlines an approach to solving the WIS problem in graphs more complicated than paths. Consider an arbitrary undirected graph $G = (V, E)$ with nonnegative vertex weights, and an arbitrary vertex $v \in V$ with weight w_v. Obtain H from G by removing v and its incident edges from G. Obtain K from H by removing v's neighbors and their incident edges:

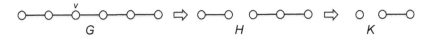

Let W_G, W_H, and W_K denote the total weight of an MWIS in G, H, and K, respectively, and consider the formula

$$W_G = \max\{W_H, W_K + w_v\}.$$

Which of the following statements are true? (Choose all that apply.)

a) The formula is not always correct in path graphs.

b) The formula is always correct in path graphs but not always correct in trees.

c) The formula is always correct in trees but not always correct in arbitrary graphs.

d) The formula is always correct in arbitrary graphs.

e) The formula leads to a linear-time algorithm for the WIS problem in trees.

f) The formula leads to a linear-time algorithm for the WIS problem in arbitrary graphs.

Problem 16.4 *(S)* Consider an instance of the knapsack problem with five items:

Item	Value	Size
1	1	1
2	2	3
3	3	2
4	4	5
5	5	4

and knapsack capacity $C = 9$. What are the final array entries of the `Knapsack` algorithm from Section 16.5, and which items belong to the optimal solution?

Challenge Problems

Problem 16.5 *(H)* This problem describes four generalizations of the knapsack problem. In each, the input consists of item values $v_1, v_2, \ldots, v_n$, item sizes $s_1, s_2, \ldots, s_n$, and additional problem-specific data (all positive integers). Which of these generalizations can be solved by dynamic programming in time polynomial in the number n of items and the largest number M that appears in the input? (Choose all that apply.)

a) Given a positive integer capacity C, compute a subset of items with the maximum-possible total value subject to having total size *exactly* C. (If no such set exists, the algorithm should correctly detect that fact.)

b) Given a positive integer capacity C and an item budget $k \in \{1, 2, \ldots, n\}$, compute a subset of items with the maximum-possible total value subject to having total size at most C *and at most k items.*

c) Given capacities C_1 and C_2 of two knapsacks, compute disjoint subsets S_1, S_2 of items with the maximum-possible total value $\sum_{i \in S_1} v_i + \sum_{i \in S_2} v_i$, subject to the knapsack capacities: $\sum_{i \in S_1} s_i \le C_1$ and $\sum_{i \in S_2} s_i \le C_2$.

d) Given capacities $C_1, C_2, \ldots, C_m$ of m knapsacks, where m could be as large as n, compute disjoint subsets $S_1, S_2, \ldots, S_m$ of items with the maximum-possible total value $\sum_{i \in S_1} v_i + \sum_{i \in S_2} v_i + \cdots + \sum_{i \in S_m} v_i$, subject to the knapsack capacities: $\sum_{i \in S_1} s_i \le C_1$, $\sum_{i \in S_2} s_i \le C_2$, $\ldots$, and $\sum_{i \in S_m} s_i \le C_m$.

Programming Problems

Problem 16.6 Implement in your favorite programming language the WIS and WIS Reconstruction algorithms. (See www.algorithmsilluminated.org for test cases and challenge data sets.)

Problem 16.7 Implement in your favorite programming language the Knapsack and Knapsack Reconstruction algorithms. (See www.algorithmsilluminated.org for test cases and challenge data sets.)

Chapter 17

Advanced Dynamic Programming

This chapter continues the dynamic programming boot camp with two more case studies: the sequence alignment problem (Section 17.1) and the problem of computing a binary search tree with the minimum-possible average search time (Section 17.2). In both cases, the structure of optimal solutions is more complex than in last chapter's case studies, with a subproblem solution depending on those from more than two smaller subproblems. After finishing this chapter, ask yourself: Could you have ever solved either problem without first studying dynamic programming?

17.1 Sequence Alignment

17.1.1 Motivation

If you take a course in computational genomics, the first few lectures will likely be devoted to the *sequence alignment* problem.[1] In this problem, the input consists of two strings that represent portions of one or more genomes, over the alphabet—no prizes for guessing!—$\{A, C, G, T\}$. The strings need not have the same length. For example, the input might be the strings $AGGGCT$ and $AGGCA$. Informally, the problem is to determine how similar the two strings are; we'll make this precise in the next section.

Why would you want to solve this problem? Here are two reasons among many. First, suppose you're trying to figure out the function of a region of a complex genome, like the human genome. One approach is to look for a similar region in a better-understood genome, like the mouse genome, and conjecture that the similar regions play the same or similar roles. A totally different application of the problem is

---

[1] The presentation in this section draws inspiration from Section 6.6 of *Algorithm Design*, by Jon Kleinberg and Éva Tardos (Pearson, 2005).

to make inferences about a phylogenetic tree—which species evolved from which, and when. For example, you might be wondering if species B evolved from species A and then species C from B, or if B and C evolved independently from A. Genome similarity can be used as a proxy for proximity in a phylogenetic tree.

17.1.2   Problem Definition

Our example strings $AGGGCT$ and $AGGCA$ are obviously not identical, but they still intuitively feel more similar than not. How can we formalize this intuition? One idea is to notice that these two strings can be "nicely aligned":

$$
\begin{array}{cccccc}
A & G & G & G & C & T \\
A & G & G & - & C & A
\end{array}
$$

where the "$-$" indicates a gap inserted between two letters of the second string, which seems to be missing a 'G'. The two strings agree in four of the six columns; the only flaws in the alignment are the gap and the mismatch between the A and T in the final column.

In general, an *alignment* is a way of inserting gaps into one or both input strings so that they have equal length:

$$
\underbrace{\begin{array}{c} \text{———————— } X + \text{gaps ————————} \\ \text{———————— } Y + \text{gaps ————————} \end{array}}_{\text{common length } \ell}
$$

We can then define the similarity of two strings according to the quality of their nicest alignment. But what makes an alignment "nice?" Is it better to have one gap and one mismatch, or three gaps and no mismatches?

Let's assume that such questions have already been answered experimentally, in the form of known *penalties* for gaps and mismatches that are provided as part of the input (along with the two strings). These specify the penalties an alignment incurs in each of its columns; the total penalty of an alignment is the sum of its columns' penalties. For example, the alignment of $AGGGCT$ and $AGGCA$ above would suffer a penalty of α_{gap} (the provided cost of a gap) plus a penalty of α_{AT} (the provided cost of an A-T mismatch). The sequence alignment problem is, then, to compute an alignment that minimizes the total penalty.

Problem: Sequence Alignment

Input: Two strings X, Y over the alphabet $\Sigma =$ $\{A, C, G, T\}$, a penalty α_{xy} for each symbol pair $x, y \in \Sigma$, and a nonnegative gap penalty $\alpha_{gap} \geq 0$.[2]

Output: An alignment of X and Y with the minimum-possible total penalty.

One way to interpret the minimum-penalty alignment is as the "most plausible explanation" of how one of the strings might have evolved into the other. We can think of a gap as undoing a deletion that occurred sometime in the past, and a mismatch as undoing a mutation.

The minimum penalty of an alignment of two strings is a famous enough concept to have its own name: the *Needleman-Wunsch* or *NW score* of the strings.[3] Two strings are then deemed "similar" if and only if their NW score is relatively small.

Quiz 17.1

Suppose there is a penalty of 1 for each gap and a penalty of 2 for matching two different symbols in a column. What is the NW score of the strings $AGTACG$ and $ACATAG$?

a) 3

b) 4

c) 5

d) 6

(See Section 17.1.8 for the solution and discussion.)

---

[2]While it's natural to assume that all penalties are nonnegative with $\alpha_{xx} = 0$ for all $x \in \Sigma$ and $\alpha_{xy} = \alpha_{yx}$ for all $x, y \in \Sigma$, our dynamic programming algorithm requires only that the gap penalty is nonnegative. (Do you see why a negative gap penalty—that is, a reward for gaps—would make the problem completely uninteresting?)

[3]Named after its inventors, Saul B. Needleman and Christian D. Wunsch, and published in the paper "A general method applicable to the search for similarities in the amino acid sequence of two proteins" (*Journal of Molecular Biology*, 1970).

The NW score would be useless to genomicists without an efficient procedure for calculating it. The number of alignments of two strings grows exponentially with their combined length, so outside of uninterestingly small instances, exhaustive search won't complete in our lifetimes. Dynamic programming will save the day; by repeating the same type of thought experiment we used for the WIS problem on path graphs and the knapsack problem, we'll arrive at an efficient algorithm for computing the NW score.[4]

17.1.3   Optimal Substructure

Rather than be unduly intimidated by how fundamental the sequence alignment problem is, let's follow our usual dynamic programming recipe and see what happens. If you've already reached black-belt status in dynamic programming, you might be able to guess the right collection of subproblems; of course, I don't expect you to be at that level after only two case studies.

Suppose someone handed us on a silver platter a minimum-penalty alignment of two strings. What must it look like? In how many different ways could it have been built up from optimal solutions to smaller subproblems? In the WIS problem on path graphs and the knapsack problem, we zoomed in on a solution's last decision—does the last vertex of the path or the last item of a knapsack instance belong to the solution? To continue the pattern, it would seem that we should zoom in on the last column of the alignment:

$$
\begin{array}{cccccc}
A & G & G & G & C & T \\
A & G & G & - & C & A
\end{array}
$$

$$
\underbrace{}_{\text{rest of alignment}} \quad \underbrace{}_{\substack{\text{last} \\ \text{column}}}
$$

In our first two case studies, the final vertex or item was either in or out of the solution—two different possibilities. In the sequence alignment problem, how many relevant possibilities are there for the contents of the final column?

---

[4]Algorithms have shaped the development of computational genomics as a field. If there *wasn't* an efficient algorithm for computing the NW score, Needleman and Wunsch surely would have proposed a different and more tractable definition of genome similarity!

Quiz 17.2

Let $X = x_1, x_2, \ldots, x_m$ and $Y = y_1, y_2, \ldots, y_n$ be two input strings, with each symbol x_i or y_j in $\{A, C, G, T\}$. How many relevant possibilities are there for the contents of the final column of an optimal alignment?

a) 2

b) 3

c) 4

d) mn

(See Section 17.1.8 for the solution and discussion.)

Following our first two case studies, the next step shows, by a case analysis, that there are only three candidates for an optimal alignment—one candidate for each of the possibilities for the contents of the last column. This will lead to a recurrence, which can be computed by exhaustive search over the three possibilities, and a dynamic programming algorithm that uses this recurrence to systematically solve all the relevant subproblems.

Consider an optimal alignment of two non-empty strings $X = x_1, x_2, \ldots, x_m$ and $Y = y_1, y_2, \ldots, y_n$. Let $X' = x_1, x_2, \ldots, x_{m-1}$ and $Y' = y_1, y_2, \ldots, y_{n-1}$ denote X and Y, respectively, with the last symbol plucked off.

Case 1: x_m and y_n matched in last column of alignment. Suppose an optimal alignment does not use a gap in its final column, preferring to match the final symbols x_m and y_n of the input strings. Let P denote the total penalty incurred by this alignment. We can view the rest of the alignment (excluding the final column) as an alignment of the remaining symbols—an alignment of the shorter strings X' and Y':

$$\underbrace{\begin{array}{cc} \underline{\hspace{4em}} X' + \text{gaps} \underline{\hspace{4em}} & x_m \\ \underline{\hspace{4em}} Y' + \text{gaps} \underline{\hspace{4em}} & y_n \end{array}}_{\text{rest of alignment}}$$

This alignment of X' and Y' has total penalty P minus the penalty $\alpha_{x_m y_n}$ that was previously paid in the last column. And it's not just any old alignment of X' and Y'—it's an *optimal* such alignment. For if some other alignment of X' and Y' had smaller total penalty $P^* < P - \alpha_{x_m y_n}$, appending to it a final column matching x_m and y_n would produce an alignment of X and Y with total penalty $P^* + \alpha_{x_m y_n} < (P - \alpha_{x_m y_n}) + \alpha_{x_m y_n} = P$, contradicting the optimality of the original alignment of X and Y.

In other words, once you know that an optimal alignment of X and Y matches x_m and y_n in its last column, you know exactly what the rest of it looks like: an optimal alignment of X' and Y'.

Case 2: x_m matched with a gap in last column of alignment.
In this case, because y_n does not appear in the last column, the induced alignment is of X' and the original second string Y:

$$
\underbrace{
\begin{array}{ccc}
\text{———} & X' + \text{gaps} & \text{———} \\
\text{———} & Y + \text{gaps} & \text{———}
\end{array}
}_{\text{rest of alignment}}
\quad
\begin{array}{c}
x_m \\
[\text{gap}].
\end{array}
$$

Moreover, the induced alignment is an optimal alignment of X' and Y; the argument is analogous to that in case 1 (as you should verify).

Case 3: y_n matched with a gap in last column of alignment.
Symmetrically, in this case, the induced alignment is of X and Y':

$$
\underbrace{
\begin{array}{ccc}
\text{———} & X + \text{gaps} & \text{———} \\
\text{———} & Y' + \text{gaps} & \text{———}
\end{array}
}_{\text{rest of alignment}}
\quad
\begin{array}{c}
[\text{gap}] \\
y_n.
\end{array}
$$

Moreover, as in the first two cases, it is an optimal such alignment (as you should verify).

The point of this case analysis is to narrow down the possibilities for an optimal solution to three and only three candidates.

Lemma 17.1 (Sequence Alignment Optimal Substructure)
An optimal alignment of two non-empty strings $X = x_1, x_2, \ldots, x_m$ and $Y = y_1, y_2, \ldots, y_n$ is either:

(i) an optimal alignment of X' and Y', supplemented with a match of x_m and y_n in the final column;

(ii) *an optimal alignment of X' and Y, supplemented with a match of x_m and a gap in the final column;*

(iii) *an optimal alignment of X and Y', supplemented with a match of a gap and y_n in the final column,*

where X' and Y' denote X and Y, respectively, with the final symbols x_m and y_n removed.

What if X or Y is the empty string?

Quiz 17.3

Suppose one of the two input strings (Y, say) is empty. What is the NW score of X and Y?

a) 0

b) $\alpha_{gap} \cdot$ (length of X)

c) $+\infty$

d) undefined

(See Section 17.1.8 for the solution and discussion.)

17.1.4   Recurrence

Quiz 17.3 handles the base case of an empty input string. For nonempty input strings, of the three options in Lemma 17.1, the one with the smallest total penalty is an optimal solution. These observations lead to the following recurrence, which computes the best of the three options by exhaustive search:

Corollary 17.2 (Sequence Alignment Recurrence) *With   the assumptions and notation of Lemma 17.1, let $P_{i,j}$ denote the total penalty of an optimal alignment of $X_i = x_1, x_2, \ldots, x_i$, the first i symbols of X, and $Y_j = y_1, y_2, \ldots, y_j$, the first j symbols of Y. (If $j = 0$ or $i = 0$, interpret $P_{i,j}$ as $i \cdot \alpha_{gap}$ or $j \cdot \alpha_{gap}$, respectively.) Then*

$$P_{m,n} = \min\{\underbrace{P_{m-1,n-1} + \alpha_{x_m y_n}}_{\text{Case 1}}, \underbrace{P_{m-1,n} + \alpha_{gap}}_{\text{Case 2}}, \underbrace{P_{m,n-1} + \alpha_{gap}}_{\text{Case 3}}\}.$$

More generally, for every $i = 1, 2, \ldots, m$ and $j = 1, 2, \ldots, n$,

$$P_{i,j} = \min\{\underbrace{P_{i-1,j-1} + \alpha_{x_i y_j}}_{Case\ 1}, \underbrace{P_{i-1,j} + \alpha_{gap}}_{Case\ 2}, \underbrace{P_{i,j-1} + \alpha_{gap}}_{Case\ 3}\}.$$

The more general statement in Corollary 17.2 follows by invoking the first statement, for each $i = 1, 2, \ldots, m$ and $j = 1, 2, \ldots, n$, with X_i and Y_j playing the role of the input strings X and Y.

17.1.5   The Subproblems

As in the knapsack problem, the subproblems in the recurrence (Corollary 17.2) are indexed by two different parameters, i and j. Knapsack subproblems can shrink in two different senses (by removing an item or removing knapsack capacity), and so it goes with sequence alignment subproblems (by removing a symbol from the first or the second input string). Ranging over all relevant values of the two parameters, we obtain our collection of subproblems:[5]

Sequence Alignment: Subproblems

Compute $P_{i,j}$, the minimum total penalty of an alignment of the first i symbols of X and the first j symbols of Y.

(For each $i = 0, 1, 2, \ldots, m$ and $j = 0, 1, 2, \ldots, n$.)

The largest subproblem (with $i = m$ and $j = n$) is exactly the same as the original problem.

17.1.6   A Dynamic Programming Algorithm

All the hard work is done. We have our subproblems. We have our recurrence for solving a subproblem given solutions to smaller subproblems. Nothing can stop us from using it to solve all the subproblems systematically, beginning with the base cases and working up to the original problem.

---

[5]Or, thinking recursively, each recursive call plucks off the last symbol from the first input string, the last symbol from the second input string, or both. The only subproblems that can arise in this way are for prefixes of the original input strings.

NW

Input: strings $X = x_1, x_2, \ldots, x_m$ and
$Y = y_1, y_2, \ldots, y_n$ over the alphabet $\Sigma = \{A, C, G, T\}$,
a penalty α_{xy} for each $x, y \in \Sigma$, and a gap penalty
$\alpha_{gap} \geq 0$.
Output: the NW score of X and Y.

```
// subproblem solutions (indexed from 0)
```
$A := (m + 1) \times (n + 1)$ two-dimensional array
```
// base case #1 (j = 0)
```
for $i = 0$ to m **do**
 $A[i][0] = i \cdot \alpha_{gap}$
```
// base case #2 (i = 0)
```
for $j = 0$ to n **do**
 $A[0][j] = j \cdot \alpha_{gap}$
```
// systematically solve all subproblems
```
for $i = 1$ to m **do**
  for $j = 1$ to n **do**
```
    // use recurrence from Corollary 17.2
```
   $A[i][j] :=$
$$\min \left\{ \begin{array}{ll} A[i-1][j-1] + \alpha_{x_i y_j} & \text{(Case 1)} \\ A[i-1][j] + \alpha_{gap} & \text{(Case 2)} \\ A[i][j-1] + \alpha_{gap} & \text{(Case 3)} \end{array} \right\}$$
 return $A[m][n]$ ```// solution to largest subproblem```

As in the knapsack problem, because subproblems are indexed by two different parameters, the algorithm uses a two-dimensional array to store subproblem solutions and a double for loop to populate it. By the time a loop iteration must compute the subproblem solution $A[i][j]$, the values $A[i-1][j-1]$, $A[i-1][j]$, and $A[i][j-1]$ of the three relevant smaller subproblems have already been computed and are ready and waiting to be looked up in constant time. This means the algorithm spends $O(1)$ time solving each of the $(m+1)(n+1) = O(mn)$ subproblems, for an overall running time of $O(mn)$.[6] Like our previous dynamic programming algorithms, correctness of the NW algorithm

---

[6] In the notation of (16.1), $f(n) = O(mn)$, $g(n) = O(1)$, and $h(n) = O(1)$.

can be proved by induction; the induction is on the value of $i + j$ (the subproblem size), with the recurrence in Corollary 17.2 justifying the inductive step.

Theorem 17.3 (Properties of NW) *For every instance of the sequence alignment problem, the NW algorithm returns the correct NW score and runs in $O(mn)$ time, where m and n are the lengths of the two input strings.*

For an example of the NW algorithm in action, check out Problem 17.1.[7]

17.1.7   Reconstruction

There are no surprises in reconstructing an optimal alignment from the array values that the NW algorithm computes. Working backward, the algorithm first checks which case of the recurrence was used to fill in the array entry $A[m][n]$ corresponding to the largest subproblem (resolving ties arbitrarily).[8] If it was case 1, the last column of the optimal alignment matches x_m and y_n and reconstruction resumes from the entry $A[m - 1][n - 1]$. If it was case 2 or 3, the last column of the alignment matches either x_m (in case 2) or y_n (in case 3) with a gap and the process resumes from the entry $A[m - 1][n]$ (in case 2) or $A[m][n - 1]$ (in case 3). When the reconstruction algorithm hits a base case, it completes the alignment by prepending the appropriate number of gaps to the string that has run out of symbols. Because the algorithm performs $O(1)$ work per iteration and each iteration decreases the sum of the lengths of the remaining prefixes, its running time is $O(m + n)$. We leave the detailed pseudocode to the interested reader.

---

[7]Can we do better? In special cases, yes (see Problem 17.6). For the general problem, cutting-edge research suggests that the answer might be "no." Intrepid readers should check out the paper "Edit Distance Cannot Be Computed in Strongly Subquadratic Time (unless SETH is false)," by Arturs Backurs and Piotr Indyk (*SIAM Journal on Computing*, 2018).

[8]Depending on the implementation details, this information may have been cached by the NW algorithm, in which case it can be looked up. (See also footnote 9 of Chapter 16.) If not, the reconstruction algorithm can recompute the answer from scratch in $O(1)$ time.

17.1.8   Solution to Quizzes 17.1–17.3

Solution to Quiz 17.1

Correct answer: (b). Here's one alignment with two gaps and one mismatch, for a total penalty of 4:

$$
\begin{array}{ccccccc}
A & - & G & T & A & C & G \\
A & C & A & T & A & - & G
\end{array}
$$

Here's one with four gaps and no mismatches, also with a total penalty of 4:

$$
\begin{array}{ccccccc}
A & - & - & G & T & A & C & G \\
A & C & A & - & T & A & - & G
\end{array}
$$

No alignment has total penalty 3 or less. Why not? Because the input strings have the same length, every alignment inserts the same number of gaps in each, and so the total number of gaps is even. An alignment with four or more gaps has total penalty at least 4. The alignment with zero gaps has four mismatches and a total penalty of 8. Every alignment that inserts only one gap in each string results in at least one mismatch, for a total penalty of at least 4.

Solution to Quiz 17.2

Correct answer: (b). Consider an optimal alignment of the strings X and Y:

$$
\underbrace{
\begin{array}{c}
\rule{3cm}{0.4pt}\; X + \text{gaps} \;\rule{3cm}{0.4pt} \\
\rule{3cm}{0.4pt}\; Y + \text{gaps} \;\rule{3cm}{0.4pt}
\end{array}
}_{\text{common length } \ell}
$$

What could reside in the upper-right corner, in the last column of the first row? It could be a gap, or it could be a symbol. If it's a symbol, it must be from X (because it's the top row) and it must be X's last symbol x_m (because it's in the last column). Similarly, the lower-right corner must be either a gap or the last symbol y_n of the second string Y.

With two choices for each of the two entries in the last column, there would seem to be four possible scenarios. But one of them is irrelevant! It's pointless to have two gaps in the same column—there's a nonnegative penalty per gap, so removing them produces a new alignment that can only be better. This leaves us with three relevant possibilities for the contents of the last column of an optimal alignment: (i) x_m and y_n are matched; (ii) x_m is matched with a gap; or (iii) y_n is matched with a gap.

Solution to Quiz 17.3

Correct answer: (b). If Y is empty, the optimal alignment inserts enough gaps into Y so that it has the same length as X. This incurs a penalty of α_{gap} per gap, for a total penalty of α_{gap} times the length of X.

*17.2 Optimal Binary Search Trees

In Chapter 11 of *Part 2* we studied binary search trees, which maintain a total ordering over an evolving set of objects and support a rich set of fast operations. In Chapter 14 we defined prefix-free codes and designed a greedy algorithm for computing the best-on-average code for a given set of symbol frequencies. Next we consider the analogous problem for search trees—computing the best-on-average search tree given statistics about the frequencies of different searches. This problem is more challenging than the optimal prefix-free code problem, but it is no match for the power of the dynamic programming paradigm.

17.2.1 Binary Search Tree Review

A *binary search tree* is a data structure that acts like a dynamic version of a sorted array—searching for an object is as easy as in a sorted array, but it also accommodates fast insertions and deletions. The data structure stores objects associated with keys (and possibly lots of other data), with one object for each node of the tree.[9] Every node has left and right child pointers, either of which can be null. The left subtree of a node x is defined as the nodes reachable from x via its left child pointer, and similarly for the right subtree. The defining *search tree property* is:

---

[9]We refer to nodes of the tree and the corresponding objects interchangeably.

The Search Tree Property

For every object x:

1. Objects in x's left subtree have keys smaller than that of x.

2. Objects in x's right subtree have keys larger than that of x.

Throughout this section, we assume, for simplicity, that no two objects have the same key.

The search tree property imposes a requirement for every node of a search tree, not just for the root:

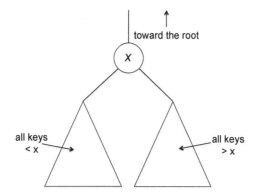

For example, here's a search tree containing objects with the keys $\{1, 2, 3, 4, 5\}$:

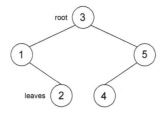

The point of the search tree property is to reduce searching for an object with a given key to following your nose, reminiscent of binary search in a sorted array. For example, suppose you're looking for an object with key 17. If the object at the root of the tree has the key 23, you know that the object you're looking for is in the root's left subtree. If the root's key is 12, you know to recursively search for the object in the right subtree.

17.2.2   Average Search Time

The *search time* for a key k in a binary search tree T is the number of nodes visited while searching for the node with key k (including that node itself). In the tree above, the key "3" has a search time of 1, the keys "1" and "5" have search times of 2, and the keys "2" and "4" have search times of 3.[10]

Different search trees for the same set of objects result in different search times. For example, here's a second search tree containing objects with the keys $\{1, 2, 3, 4, 5\}$:

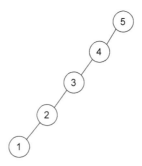

where the "1" now has a search time of 5.

Of all the search trees for a given set of objects, which is the "best?" We asked this question in Chapter 11 of *Part 2*, and the answer there was a perfectly balanced tree:

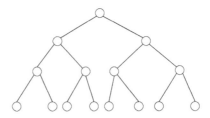

The rationale? A perfectly balanced tree minimizes the length of the longest root-leaf path ($\approx \log_2 n$ for n objects) or, equivalently, the maximum search time. Balanced binary search tree data structures,

---

[10]Equivalently, the search time is one plus the depth of the corresponding node in the tree.

such as red-black trees, are explicitly designed to keep the search tree close to perfectly balanced (see Section 11.4 of *Part 2*).

Minimizing the maximum search time makes sense when you don't have advance knowledge about which searches are more likely than others. But what if you have statistics about the frequencies of different searches?[11]

Quiz 17.4

Consider the following two search trees that store objects with keys 1, 2, and 3:

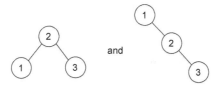

and the search frequencies:

Key	Search Frequency
1	.8
2	.1
3	.1

What are the average search times in the two trees, respectively?

a) 1.9 and 1.2

b) 1.9 and 1.3

c) 2 and 1

d) 2 and 3

(See Section 17.2.9 for the solution and discussion.)

---

[11]For example, imagine you implement a spell checker as a binary search tree that stores all the correctly spelled words. Spell-checking a document reduces to looking up each of its words in turn, with unsuccessful searches corresponding to misspelled words. You can estimate the frequencies of different searches by counting the number of occurrences of different words (both correctly and incorrectly spelled) in a sufficiently large set of representative documents.

17.2.3   Problem Definition

Quiz 17.4 shows that the best binary search tree for the job depends on the search frequencies, with unbalanced trees potentially superior to balanced trees when the search frequencies are not uniform. This observation suggests a cool opportunity for algorithm design: Given the search frequencies for a set of keys, what's the best binary search tree?

Problem: Optimal Binary Search Trees

Input: A sorted list of keys $k_1, k_2, \ldots, k_n$ and a nonnegative frequency p_i for each key k_i.

Output: The binary search tree T containing the keys $\{k_1, k_2, \ldots, k_n\}$ with minimum-possible weighted search time:

$$\sum_{i=1}^{n} p_i \cdot \underbrace{(\text{search time for } k_i \text{ in } T)}_{=(k_i\text{'s depth in } T)+1}. \qquad (17.1)$$

Three comments. First, the names of the keys are not important, so among friends let's just call them $\{1, 2, \ldots, n\}$. Second, the problem formulation does not assume that the p_i's sum to 1 (hence the phrasing "weighted" search time instead of "average" search time). If this bothers you, feel free to normalize the frequencies by dividing each of them by their sum $\sum_{j=1}^{n} p_j$—this doesn't change the problem. Third, the problem as stated is unconcerned with unsuccessful searches, meaning searches for a key other than one in the given set $\{k_1, k_2, \ldots, k_n\}$. You should check that our dynamic programming solution extends to the case in which unsuccessful search times are also counted, provided the input specifies the frequencies of such searches.

The optimal binary search tree problem bears some resemblance to the optimal prefix-free code problem (Chapter 14). In both problems, the input specifies a set of frequencies over symbols or keys, the output is a binary tree, and the objective function is related to minimizing the average depth. The difference lies in the constraint that the binary tree must satisfy. In the optimal prefix-free code problem, the sole restriction is that symbols appear only at the leaves. A solution to the optimal binary search tree problem must satisfy the more challenging search tree property (page 149). This is why greedy algorithms aren't good enough for the latter problem; we'll need to up our game and apply the dynamic programming paradigm.

17.2.4   Optimal Substructure

The first step, as always with dynamic programming, is to understand the ways in which an optimal solution might be built up from optimal solutions to smaller subproblems. As a warm-up, suppose we took a (doomed-to-fail) divide-and-conquer approach to the optimal binary search tree problem. Every recursive call of a divide-and-conquer algorithm commits to a single split of its problem into one or more smaller subproblems. Which split should we use? A first thought might be to install the object with the median key at the root, and then recursively compute the left and right subtrees. With non-uniform search frequencies, however, there's no reason to expect the median to be a good choice for the root (see Quiz 17.4). The choice of root has unpredictable repercussions further down the tree, so how could we know in advance the right way to split the problem into two smaller subproblems? If only we had clairvoyance and knew which key should appear at the root, we might then be able to compute the rest of the tree recursively.

If only we knew the root. This is starting to sound familiar. In the WIS problem on path graphs (Section 16.2.1), if only you knew whether the last vertex belonged to an optimal solution, you would know what the rest of it looked like. In the knapsack problem (Section 16.5.2), if only you knew whether the last item belonged to an optimal solution, you would know what the rest of it looked like. In the sequence alignment problem (Section 17.1.3), if only you knew the contents of the final column of an optimal alignment, you would know what the rest of it looked like. How did we overcome our ignorance? By trying all the possibilities—two possibilities in the WIS and knapsack problems, and three in the sequence alignment problem. Reasoning by analogy, perhaps our solution to the optimal binary search tree problem should *try all the possible roots.*

With this in mind, the next quiz asks you to guess what type of optimal substructure lemma might be true for the optimal binary search tree problem.

Quiz 17.5

Suppose an optimal binary search tree for the keys
$\{1, 2, \ldots, n\}$ and frequencies $p_1, p_2, \ldots, p_n$ has the key r
at its root, with left subtree T_1 and right subtree T_2:

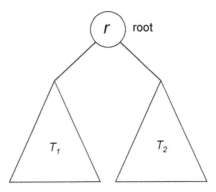

Of the following four statements, choose the strongest one
that you suspect is true.

a) Neither T_1 nor T_2 need be optimal for the keys it
   contains.

b) At least one of T_1, T_2 is optimal for the keys it contains.

c) Each of T_1, T_2 is optimal for the keys it contains.

d) T_1 is an optimal binary search tree for the keys
   $\{1, 2, \ldots, r - 1\}$, and similarly T_2 for the keys $\{r +
   1, r + 2, \ldots, n\}$.

(See Section 17.2.9 for the solution and discussion.)

As usual, formalizing the optimal substructure boils down to a
case analysis, with one case for each possibility of what an optimal
solution might look like. Consider an optimal binary search tree T
with keys $\{1, 2, \ldots, n\}$ and frequencies $p_1, p_2, \ldots, p_n$. Any of the n
keys might appear at the root of an optimal solution, so there are n
different cases. We can reason about all of them in one fell swoop.

Case r: The root of T has key r. Let T_1 and T_2 denote the left
and right subtrees of the root. The search tree property implies that

the residents of T_1 are the keys $\{1, 2, \ldots, r-1\}$, and similarly for T_2 and $\{r+1, r+2, \ldots, n\}$. Moreover, T_1 and T_2 are both valid search trees for their sets of keys (i.e., both T_1 and T_2 satisfy the search tree property). We next show that both are *optimal* binary search trees for their respective subproblems, with the frequencies $p_1, p_2, \ldots, p_{r-1}$ and $p_{r+1}, p_{r+2}, \ldots, p_n$ inherited from the original problem.[12]

Suppose, for contradiction, that at least one of the subtrees—T_1, say—is not an optimal solution to its corresponding subproblem. This means there is a different search tree T_1^* with keys $\{1, 2, \ldots, r-1\}$ and with strictly smaller weighted search time:

$$\sum_{k=1}^{r-1} p_k \cdot (k\text{'s search time in } T_1^*) < \sum_{k=1}^{r-1} p_k \cdot (k\text{'s search time in } T_1). \quad (17.2)$$

From our previous case studies, we know what we must do next: Use the inequality (17.2) to exhibit a search tree for the original problem superior to T, thereby contradicting the purported optimality of T. We can obtain such a tree T^* by performing surgery on T, cutting out its left subtree T_1 and pasting T_1^* in its place:

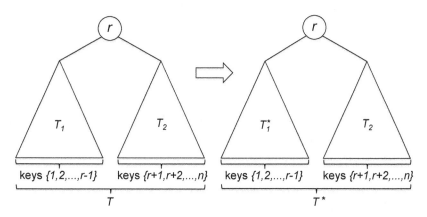

The final step is to compare the weighted search times in T^* and T. Splitting the sum in (17.1) into two parts, the keys $\{1, 2, \ldots, r-1\}$ and the keys $\{r, r+1, \ldots, n\}$, we can write these search times as

$$\sum_{k=1}^{r-1} p_k \cdot \underbrace{(k\text{'s search time in } T^*)}_{=1+(\text{search time in } T_1^*)} + \sum_{k=r}^{n} p_k \cdot (k\text{'s search time in } T^*)$$

---

[12]No worries if $r = 1$ or $r = n$; in that case, one of the two subtrees is empty, and the empty tree is trivially optimal for the empty set of keys.

and

$$\sum_{k=1}^{r-1} \underbrace{p_k \cdot (k\text{'s search time in } T)}_{=1+(\text{search time in } T_1)} + \sum_{k=r}^{n} p_k \cdot \underbrace{(k\text{'s search time in } T)}_{\text{same as in } T^* \text{ (as } k \geq r)},$$

respectively. Because the trees T^* and T have the same root r and the same right subtree T_2, the search times for the keys $r, r+1, \ldots, n$ are the same in both trees. A search for a key in $\{1, 2, \ldots, r-1\}$ first visits the root r and then recursively searches the left subtree. Thus, the search time for such a key is one more in T^* than in T_1^*, and one more in T than in T_1. This means the weighted search times in T^* and T can be written as

$$\underbrace{\sum_{k=1}^{r-1} p_k \cdot (k\text{'s search time in } T_1^*) + \sum_{k=1}^{r-1} p_k}_{\text{left-hand side of (17.2)}} + \sum_{k=r}^{n} p_k \cdot (k\text{'s search time in } T^*)$$

and

$$\underbrace{\sum_{k=1}^{r-1} p_k \cdot (k\text{'s search time in } T_1) + \sum_{k=1}^{r-1} p_k}_{\text{right-hand side of (17.2)}} + \sum_{k=r}^{n} p_k \cdot (k\text{'s search time in } T^*),$$

respectively. The second and third terms are the same in both expressions. Our assumption (17.2) is that the first term is smaller in the first expression than in the second, which implies that the weighted search time in T^* is smaller than that in T. This furnishes the promised contradiction and completes the proof of the key claim that T_1 and T_2 are optimal binary search trees for their respective subproblems.

Lemma 17.4 (Optimal BST Optimal Substructure) *If T is an optimal binary search tree with keys $\{1, 2, \ldots, n\}$, frequencies $p_1, p_2, \ldots, p_n$, root r, left subtree T_1, and right subtree T_2, then:*

(a) T_1 is an optimal binary search tree for the keys $\{1, 2, \ldots, r-1\}$ and frequencies $p_1, p_2, \ldots, p_{r-1}$; and

(b) T_2 is an optimal binary search tree for the keys $\{r+1, r+2, \ldots, n\}$ and frequencies $p_{r+1}, p_{r+2}, \ldots, p_n$.

In other words, once you know the root of an optimal binary search tree, you know exactly what its left and right subtrees look like.

17.2.5   Recurrence

Lemma 17.4 narrows down the possibilities for an optimal binary search tree to n and only n candidates, where n is the number of keys in the input (i.e., the number of options for the root). The best of these n candidates must be an optimal solution.

Corollary 17.5 (Optimal BST Recurrence) *With the assumptions and notation of Lemma 17.4, let $W_{i,j}$ denote the weighted search time of an optimal binary search tree with the keys $\{i, i+1, \ldots, j\}$ and frequencies $p_i, p_{i+1}, \ldots, p_j$. (If $i > j$, interpret $W_{i,j}$ as 0.) Then*

$$W_{1,n} = \sum_{k=1}^{n} p_k + \min_{r \in \{1,2,\ldots,n\}} \underbrace{\{W_{1,r-1} + W_{r+1,n}\}}_{Case\ r}. \qquad (17.3)$$

More generally, for every $i, j \in \{1, 2, \ldots, n\}$ with $i \leq j$,

$$W_{i,j} = \sum_{k=i}^{j} p_k + \min_{r \in \{i,i+1,\ldots,j\}} \underbrace{\{W_{i,r-1} + W_{r+1,j}\}}_{Case\ r}.$$

The more general statement in Corollary 17.5 follows by invoking the first statement, for each $i, j \in \{1, 2, \ldots, n\}$ with $i \leq j$, with the keys $\{i, i+1, \ldots, j\}$ and their frequencies playing the role of the original input.

The "min" in the recurrence (17.3) implements the exhaustive search through the n different candidates for an optimal solution. The term $\sum_{k=1}^{n} p_k$ is necessary because installing the optimal subtrees under a new root adds 1 to all their keys' search times.[13] As a sanity check, note that this extra term is needed for the recurrence to be correct even when there is only one key (and the weighted search time is the frequency of that key).

---

[13]In more detail, consider a tree T with root r and left and right subtrees T_1 and T_2. The search times for the keys $\{1, 2, \ldots, r-1\}$ in T are one more than in T_1, and those for the keys $\{r+1, r+2, \ldots, n\}$ in T are one more than in T_2. Thus, the weighted search time (17.1) can be written as $\sum_{k=1}^{r-1} p_k \cdot (1 + k\text{'s search time in } T_1) + p_r \cdot 1 + \sum_{k=r+1}^{n} p_k \cdot (1 + k\text{'s search time in } T_2)$, which cleans up to $\sum_{k=1}^{n} p_k + (\text{weighted search time in } T_1) + (\text{weighted search time in } T_2)$.

17.2.6   The Subproblems

In the knapsack problem (Section 16.5.3), subproblems were indexed by two parameters because the "size" of a subproblem was
two-dimensional (with one parameter tracking the prefix of items
and the other tracking the remaining knapsack capacity). Similarly,
in the sequence alignment problem (Section 17.1.5), there was one
parameter tracking the prefix of each of the two input strings. Eye-
balling the recurrence in Corollary 17.5, we see that subproblems are
again indexed by two parameters (i and j), but this time for different
reasons. Subproblems of the form $W_{1,r-1}$ in the recurrence (17.3) are
defined by prefixes of the set of keys (as usual), but subproblems of
the form $W_{r+1,n}$ are defined by *suffixes* of the keys. To be prepared
for both cases, we must keep track of both the first (smallest) and
last (largest) keys that belong to a subproblem.[14] We therefore end
up with a two-dimensional set of subproblems, despite the seemingly
one-dimensional input.

Ranging over all relevant values of the two parameters, we obtain
our collection of subproblems.

Optimal BST: Subproblems

Compute $W_{i,j}$, the minimum weighted search time of a
binary search tree with keys $\{i, i+1, \ldots, j\}$ and frequencies $p_i, p_{i+1}, \ldots, p_j$.

(For each $i, j \in \{1, 2, \ldots, n\}$ with $i \leq j$.)

The largest subproblem (with $i = 1$ and $j = n$) is exactly the same as
the original problem.

---

[14]Or, thinking recursively, each recursive call throws away either one or more
of the smallest keys, or one or more of the largest keys. The subproblems that
can arise in this way correspond to the contiguous subsets of the original set of
keys—sets of the form $\{i, i+1, \ldots, j\}$ for some $i, j \in \{1, 2, \ldots, n\}$ with $i \leq j$. For
example, a recursive call might be given a prefix of the original input $\{1, 2, \ldots, 100\}$,
such as $\{1, 2, \ldots, 22\}$, but some of its own recursive calls will be on suffixes of its
input, such as $\{18, 19, 20, 21, 22\}$.

17.2.7   A Dynamic Programming Algorithm

With the subproblems and recurrence in hand, you should expect the dynamic programming algorithm to write itself. The one detail to get right is the order in which to solve the subproblems. The simplest way to define "subproblem size" is as the number of keys in the input. Therefore, it makes sense to first solve all the subproblems with a single-key input, then the subproblems with two keys in the input, and so on. In the following pseudocode, the variable s controls the current subproblem size.[15]

OptBST

Input: keys $\{1, 2, \ldots, n\}$ with nonnegative frequencies $p_1, p_2, \ldots, p_n$.
Output: the minimum weighted search time (17.1) of a binary search tree with the keys $\{1, 2, \ldots, n\}$.

```
// subproblems (i indexed from 1, j from 0)
A := (n + 1) × (n + 1) two-dimensional array
// base cases (i = j + 1)
for i = 1 to n + 1 do
    A[i][i − 1] := 0
// systematically solve all subproblems (i ≤ j)
for s = 0 to n − 1 do        // s=subproblem size-1
    for i = 1 to n − s do    // i + s plays role of j
        // use recurrence from Corollary 17.5
        A[i][i + s] :=
            ∑_{k=i}^{i+s} p_k + min_{r=i}^{i+s} { A[i][r − 1] + A[r + 1][i + s] }
                                              ────────────────────────────
                                                       Case r
return A[1][n] // solution to largest subproblem
```

In the loop iteration responsible for computing the subproblem solution $A[i][i + s]$, all the terms of the form $A[i][r − 1]$ and $A[r + 1][i + s]$ correspond to solutions of smaller subproblems computed in earlier iterations of the outer for loop (or in the base cases). These values are ready and waiting to be looked up in constant time.

---

[15]For an example of the algorithm in action, see Problem 17.4.

Pictorially, we can visualize the array A in the `OptBST` algorithm as a two-dimensional table, with each iteration of the outer for loop corresponding to a diagonal and with the inner for loop filling in the diagonal's entries from "southwest" to "northeast":

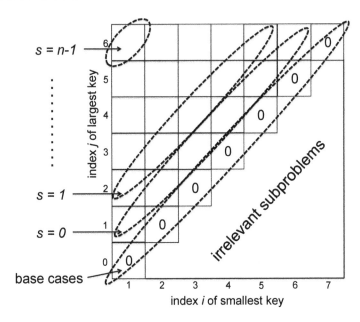

During the computation of an array entry $A[i][i+s]$, all the relevant terms of the form $A[i][r-1]$ and $A[r+1][i+s]$ lie on (previously computed) lower diagonals.

As with all our dynamic programming algorithms, the correctness of the `OptBST` algorithm follows by induction (on the subproblem size), with the recurrence in Corollary 17.5 justifying the inductive step.

What about the running time? Don't be fooled into thinking that the line of pseudocode performed in each loop iteration translates into a constant number of primitive computer operations. Computing the sum $\sum_{k=i}^{i+s} p_k$ and exhaustively searching through the $s+1$ cases of the recurrence takes $O(s) = O(n)$ time.[16] There are $O(n^2)$ iterations (one per subproblem), for an overall running time of $O(n^3)$.[17]

---

[16]Can you think of an optimization that avoids computing the sum $\sum_{k=i}^{i+s} p_k$ from scratch for each of the subproblems?

[17]In the notation of (16.1), $f(n) = O(n^2)$, $g(n) = O(n)$, and $h(n) = O(1)$. This is our first case study in which the per-subproblem work $g(n)$ is not bounded by a constant.

Theorem 17.6 (Properties of OptBST) *For every set* $\{1, 2, \ldots, n\}$ *of keys and nonnegative frequencies* $p_1, p_2, \ldots, p_n$, *the* OptBST *algorithm runs in* $O(n^3)$ *time and returns the minimum weighted search time of a binary search tree with keys* $\{1, 2, \ldots, n\}$.

Analogous to our other case studies, an optimal binary search tree can be reconstructed by tracing back through the final array A computed by the OptBST algorithm.[18]

17.2.8   Improving the Running Time

The cubic running time of the OptBST algorithm certainly does not qualify as blazingly fast. The first piece of good news is that the algorithm is way faster than exhaustively searching through all (exponentially many) binary search trees. The algorithm is fast enough to solve problems with n in the hundreds in a reasonable amount of time, but not problems with n in the thousands. The second piece of good news is that a slight tweak to the algorithm brings its running time down to $O(n^2)$.[19] This is fast enough to solve problems with n

---

[18]If the OptBST algorithm is modified to cache the roots that determine the recurrence values for each subproblem (i.e., the value of r such that $A[i][i + s] = A[i][r - 1] + A[r + 1][i + s]$), the reconstruction algorithm runs in $O(n)$ time (as you should verify). Otherwise, it must recompute these roots and runs in $O(n^2)$ time.

[19]Here's the idea. First, compute in advance all sums of the form $\sum_{k=i}^{j} p_k$; this can be done in $O(n^2)$ time (do you see how?). Then, along with each subproblem solution $A[i][j]$, store the choice of the root $r(i, j)$ that minimizes $A[i][r - 1] + A[r + 1][j]$ or, equivalently, the root of an optimal search tree for the subproblem. (If there are multiple such roots, use the smallest one.)

The key lemma is an easy-to-believe (but tricky-to-prove) monotonicity property: Adding a new maximum (respectively, minimum) element to a subproblem can only make the root of an optimal search tree larger (respectively, smaller). Intuitively, any change in the root should be in service of rebalancing the total frequency of keys between its left and right subtrees.

Assuming this lemma, for every subproblem with $i < j$, the optimal root $r(i, j)$ is at least $r(i, j - 1)$ and at most $r(i + 1, j)$. (If $i = j$, then $r(i, j)$ must be i.) Thus, there's no point in exhaustively searching all the roots between i and j—the roots between $r(i, j - 1)$ and $r(i + 1, j)$ suffice. In the worst case, there could be as many as n such roots. In aggregate over all $\Theta(n^2)$ subproblems, however, the number of roots examined is $\sum_{i=1}^{n-1} \sum_{j=i+1}^{n} (r(i + 1, j) - r(i, j - 1) + 1)$, which after cancellations is only $O(n^2)$ (as you should check). For further details, see the paper "Optimum Binary Search Trees," by Donald E. Knuth (*Acta Informatica*, 1971).

in the thousands and perhaps even tens of thousands in a reasonable amount of time.

17.2.9   Solution to Quizzes 17.4–17.5

Solution to Quiz 17.4

Correct answer: (b). For the first search tree, the "1" contributes $.8 \times 2 = 1.6$ to the average search time (because its frequency is .8 and its search time is 2), the "2" contributes $.1 \times 1 = .1$, and the "3" contributes $.1 \times 2 = .2$, for a total of $1.6 + .1 + .2 = 1.9$.

The second search tree has a larger maximum search time (3 instead of 2), but the lucky case of a search for the root is now much more likely. The "1" now contributes $.8 \times 1 = .8$ to the average search time, the "2" contributes $.1 \times 2 = .2$, and the "3" contributes $.1 \times 3 = .3$, for a total of $.8 + .2 + .3 = 1.3$.

Solution to Quiz 17.5

Correct answer: (d). Our vision is of a dynamic programming algorithm that tries all possibilities for the root, recursively computing or looking up the optimal left and right subtrees for each possibility. This strategy would be hopeless unless the left and right subtrees of an optimal binary search tree were guaranteed to be optimal in their own right for the corresponding subproblems. Thus, for our approach to succeed, the answer should be either (c) or (d). Moreover, by the search tree property, given the root r we know the demographics of its two subtrees—the keys less than r belong to the root's left subtree, and those greater than r to its right subtree.

The Upshot

★ In the sequence alignment problem, the input comprises two strings and penalties for gaps and mismatches, and the goal is to compute an alignment of the two strings with the minimum-possible total penalty.

★ The sequence alignment problem can be solved using dynamic programming in $O(mn)$ time, where m and n are the lengths of the input strings.

☆ Subproblems correspond to prefixes of the two input strings. There are three different ways in which an optimal solution can be built from optimal solutions to smaller subproblems, resulting in a recurrence with three cases.

☆ In the optimal binary search tree problem, the input is a set of n keys and nonnegative frequencies for them, and the goal is to compute a binary search tree containing these keys with the minimum-possible weighted search time.

☆ The optimal binary search tree problem can be solved using dynamic programming in $O(n^3)$ time, where n is the number of keys. A slight tweak to the algorithm reduces the running time to $O(n^2)$.

☆ Subproblems correspond to contiguous subsets of the input keys. There are n different ways in which an optimal solution can be built from optimal solutions to smaller subproblems, resulting in a recurrence with n cases.

Test Your Understanding

Problem 17.1 *(S)* For the sequence alignment input in Quiz 17.1, what are the final array entries of the NW algorithm from Section 17.1?

Problem 17.2 *(H)* The Knapsack algorithm from Section 16.5 and the NW algorithm from Section 17.1 both fill in a two-dimensional array using a double for loop. Suppose we reverse the order of the for loops—literally cutting and pasting the second loop in front of the first, without changing the pseudocode in any other way. Are the resulting algorithms well defined and correct?

a) Neither algorithm remains well defined and correct after reversing the order of the for loops.

b) Both algorithms remain well defined and correct after reversing the order of the for loops.

c) The `Knapsack` algorithm remains well defined and correct after reversing the order of the for loops, but the `NW` algorithm does not.

d) The `NW` algorithm remains well defined and correct after reversing the order of the for loops, but the `Knapsack` algorithm does not.

Problem 17.3 *(S)* The following problems all take as input two strings X and Y, with lengths m and n, over some alphabet Σ. Which of them can be solved in $O(mn)$ time? (Choose all that apply.)

a) Consider the variation of sequence alignment in which, instead of a single gap penalty α_{gap}, you are given two positive numbers a and b. The penalty for inserting k gaps in a row is now defined as $ak+b$, rather than $k \cdot \alpha_{gap}$. The other penalties (for matching two symbols) are defined as before. The goal is to compute the minimum-possible penalty of an alignment under this new cost model.

b) Compute the length of a longest common subsequence of X and Y. (A subsequence need not comprise consecutive symbols. For example, the longest common subsequence of "abcdef" and "afebcd" is "abcd.")[20]

c) Assume that X and Y have the same length n. Determine whether there exists a permutation f, mapping each $i \in \{1, 2, \ldots, n\}$ to a distinct value $f(i) \in \{1, 2, \ldots, n\}$, such that $X_i = Y_{f(i)}$ for every $i = 1, 2, \ldots, n$.

d) Compute the length of a longest common substring of X and Y. (A substring is a subsequence comprising consecutive symbols. For example, "bcd" is a substring of "abcdef," while "bdf" is not.)

---

[20] A dynamic programming algorithm for the longest common subsequence problem underlies the `diff` command familiar to users of Unix and Git.

Problem 17.4 *(S)* Consider an instance of the optimal binary search tree problem with keys $\{1, 2, \ldots, 7\}$ and the following frequencies:

Symbol	Frequency
1	20
2	5
3	17
4	10
5	20
6	3
7	25

What are the final array entries of the OptBST algorithm from Section 17.2?

Problem 17.5 *(H)* Recall the WIS algorithm (Section 16.2), the NW algorithm (Section 17.1), and the OptBST algorithm (Section 17.2). The space requirements of these algorithms are proportional to the number of subproblems: $\Theta(n)$, where n is the number of vertices; $\Theta(mn)$, where m and n are the lengths of the input strings; and $\Theta(n^2)$, where n is the number of keys, respectively.

Suppose we only want to compute the value of an optimal solution and don't care about reconstruction. How much space do you then really need to run each of the three algorithms, respectively?

a) $\Theta(1)$, $\Theta(1)$, and $\Theta(n)$

b) $\Theta(1)$, $\Theta(n)$, and $\Theta(n)$

c) $\Theta(1)$, $\Theta(n)$, and $\Theta(n^2)$

d) $\Theta(n)$, $\Theta(n)$, and $\Theta(n^2)$

Challenge Problems

Problem 17.6 *(H)* In the sequence alignment problem, suppose you knew that the input strings were relatively similar, in the sense that there is an optimal alignment that uses at most k gaps, where k is much smaller than the lengths m and n of the strings. Show how to compute the NW score in $O((m+n)k)$ time.

Problem 17.7 *(H)* There are seven kinds of Tetris pieces.[21] Design a dynamic programming algorithm that, given $x_1, x_2, \ldots, x_7$ copies of each respective piece, determines whether you can tile a 10-by-n board with exactly those pieces (placing them however and wherever you want—not necessarily in Tetris order). The running time of your algorithm should be polynomial in n.

Programming Problems

Problem 17.8 Implement in your favorite programming language the NW and OptBST algorithms, along with their reconstruction algorithms. (See www.algorithmsilluminated.org for test cases and challenge data sets.)

---

[21] See https://www.tetrisfriends.com/help/tips_beginner.php.

Chapter 18

Shortest Paths Revisited

This chapter centers around two famous dynamic programming algorithms for computing shortest paths in a graph. Both are slower but more general than Dijkstra's shortest-path algorithm (covered in Chapter 9 of *Part 2*, and similar to Prim's algorithm in Sections 15.2–15.4). The Bellman-Ford algorithm (Section 18.2) solves the single-source shortest path problem with negative edge lengths; it also has the benefit of being "more distributed" than Dijkstra's algorithm and, for this reason, has deeply influenced the way in which traffic is routed in the Internet. The Floyd-Warshall algorithm (Section 18.4) also accommodates negative edge lengths and computes shortest-path distances from *every* origin to every destination.

18.1 Shortest Paths with Negative Edge Lengths

18.1.1 The Single-Source Shortest-Path Problem

In the single-source shortest path problem, the input consists of a directed graph $G = (V, E)$ with a real-valued length ℓ_e for each edge $e \in E$ and a designated origin $s \in V$, which is called the *source vertex* or *starting vertex*. The *length* of a path is the sum of the lengths of its edges. The responsibility of an algorithm is to compute, for every possible destination v, the minimum length $dist(s, v)$ of a directed path in G from s to v. (If no such path exists, $dist(s, v)$ is defined as $+\infty$.) For example, the shortest-path distances from s in the graph

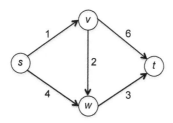

are $dist(s, s) = 0$, $dist(s, v) = 1$, $dist(s, w) = 3$, and $dist(s, t) = 6$.

Problem: Single-Source Shortest Paths
(Preliminary Version)

Input: A directed graph $G = (V, E)$, a source vertex $s \in V$, and a real-valued length ℓ_e for each edge $e \in E$.[1]

Output: the shortest-path distance $dist(s, v)$ for every vertex $v \in V$.

For example, if every edge e has unit length $\ell_e = 1$, a shortest path minimizes the hop count (i.e., number of edges) between its origin and destination.[2] Or, if the graph represents a road network and the length of each edge the expected travel time from one end to the other, the single-source shortest path problem is the problem of computing driving times from an origin (the source vertex) to all possible destinations.

Readers of *Part 2* learned a blazingly fast algorithm, Dijkstra's algorithm, for the special case of the single-source shortest path problem in which every edge length ℓ_e is nonnegative.[3] Dijkstra's algorithm, great as it is, is *not* always correct in graphs with negative edge lengths. It fails even in a trivial example like:

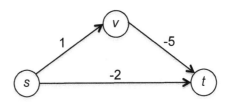

---

[1] As with the minimum spanning tree problem, we can assume that the input graph has no parallel edges. If there are multiple edges with the same beginning and end, we can throw away all but the shortest one without changing the problem.

[2] This special case of the single-source shortest path problem can be solved in linear time using breadth-first search; see Section 8.2 of *Part 2*.

[3] Analogous to Prim's algorithm (Section 15.3), a heap-based implementation of Dijkstra's algorithm runs in $O((m + n) \log n)$ time, where m and n denote the number of edges and vertices of the input graph, respectively.

If we want to accommodate negative edge lengths, we'll need a new shortest-path algorithm.[4]

18.1.2   Negative Cycles

Who cares about negative edge lengths? In many applications, like computing driving directions, edge lengths are automatically nonnegative (barring a time machine) and there's nothing to worry about. But remember that paths in a graph can represent abstract sequences of decisions. For example, perhaps you want to compute a profitable sequence of financial transactions that involves both buying and selling. This problem corresponds to finding a shortest path in a graph with edge lengths that are both positive and negative.

With negative edge lengths, we must be careful about what we even *mean* by "shortest-path distance." It's clear enough in the three-vertex example above, with $dist(s, s) = 0$, $dist(s, v) = 1$, and $dist(s, t) = -4$. What about in a graph like the following?

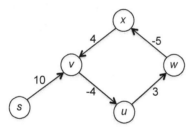

The issue is that this graph has a *negative cycle*, meaning a directed cycle in which the sum of its edges' lengths is negative. What might we mean by a "shortest s-v path?"

Option #1: Allow cycles. The first option is to allow s-v paths that include one or more cycles. But then, in the presence of a negative cycle, a "shortest path" need not even exist! For example, in the graph above, there is a one-hop s-v path with length 10. Tacking a cycle traversal at the end produces a five-hop s-v path with total length 8. Adding a second traversal increases the number of hops to 9 but decreases the overall length to 6... and so on, ad infinitum.

---

[4]You cannot reduce the single-source shortest path problem with general edge lengths to the special case of nonnegative edge lengths by adding a large positive constant to the length of every edge. In the three-vertex example above, adding 5 to every edge length would change the shortest path from $s \to v \to t$ to $s \to t$.

Thus, there is no shortest s-v path, and the only sensible definition of $dist(s, v)$ is $-\infty$.

Option #2: Forbid cycles. What if we consider only paths without cycles? With no repeat vertices allowed, we have only a finite number of paths to worry about. The "shortest s-v path" would then be whichever one has the smallest length. This definition makes perfect sense, but there's a more subtle problem: In the presence of a negative cycle, this version of the single-source shortest path problem is what's called an "NP-hard problem." *Part 4* discusses such problems at length; for now, all you need to know is that NP-hard problems, unlike almost all the problems we've studied so far in this book series, do not seem to admit any algorithm that is guaranteed to be correct and to run in polynomial time.[5]

Both options are disasters, so should we give up? Never! Even if we concede that negative cycles are problematic, we can aspire to solve the single-source shortest path problem in instances that have no negative cycles, such as the three-vertex example on page 168. This brings us to the revised version of the single-source shortest path problem.

Problem: Single-Source Shortest Paths (Revised Version)

Input: A directed graph $G = (V, E)$, a source vertex $s \in V$, and a real-valued length ℓ_e for each edge $e \in E$.

Output: One of the following:

(i) the shortest-path distance $dist(s, v)$ for every vertex $v \in V$; or

(ii) a declaration that G contains a negative cycle.

Thus, we're after an algorithm that either computes the correct shortest-path distances or offers a compelling excuse for its failure (in

---

[5]More precisely, any polynomial-time algorithm for any NP-hard problem would disprove the famous "$P \neq NP$" conjecture and resolve what is arguably the most important open question in all of computer science. See *Part 4* for the full story.

the form of a negative cycle). Any such algorithm returns the correct shortest-path distances in input graphs without negative cycles.[6]

Suppose a graph has no negative cycles. What does that buy us?

Quiz 18.1

Consider an instance of the single-source shortest path problem with n vertices, m edges, a source vertex s, and no negative cycles. Which of the following is true? (Choose the strongest true statement.)

a) For every vertex v reachable from the source s, there is a shortest s-v path with at most $n - 1$ edges.

b) For every vertex v reachable from the source s, there is a shortest s-v path with at most n edges.

c) For every vertex v reachable from the source s, there is a shortest s-v path with at most m edges.

d) There is no finite upper bound (as a function of n and m) on the fewest number of edges in a shortest s-v path.

(See Section 18.1.3 for the solution and discussion.)

18.1.3   Solution to Quiz 18.1

Correct answer: (a). If you give me a path P between the source vertex s and some destination vertex v containing at least n edges, I can give you back another s-v path P' with fewer edges than P and length no longer than that of P. This assertion implies that any s-v path can be converted into an s-v path with at most $n - 1$ edges that is only shorter; hence, there is a shortest s-v path with at most $n - 1$ edges.

---

[6]For example, suppose the edges of the input graph and their lengths represent financial transactions and their costs, with vertices corresponding to different asset portfolios. Then, a negative cycle corresponds to an arbitrage opportunity. In many cases there will be no such opportunities; if there is one, you'd be very happy to identify it!

To see why this assertion is true, observe that a path P with at least n edges visits at least $n+1$ vertices and thus makes a repeat visit to some vertex w.[7] Splicing out the cyclic subpath between successive visits to w produces a path P' with the same endpoints as P but fewer edges; see also Figure 15.2 and footnote 4 in Chapter 15. The length of P' is the same as that of P, less the sum of the edge lengths in the spliced-out cycle. *Because the input graph has no negative cycles*, this sum is nonnegative and the length of P' is less than or equal to that of P.

18.2   The Bellman-Ford Algorithm

The Bellman-Ford algorithm solves the single-source shortest path problem in graphs with negative edge lengths in the sense that it either computes the correct shortest-path distances or correctly determines that the input graph has a negative cycle.[8] This algorithm will follow naturally from the design pattern that we used in our other dynamic programming case studies.

18.2.1   The Subproblems

As always with dynamic programming, the most important step is to understand the different ways that an optimal solution might be built up from optimal solutions to smaller subproblems. Formulating the right measure of subproblem size can be tricky for graph problems. Your first guess might be that subproblems should correspond to subgraphs of the original input graph, with subproblem size equal to the number of vertices or edges in the subgraph. This idea worked well in the WIS problem on path graphs (Section 16.2), in which the vertices were inherently ordered and it was relatively clear which subgraphs to focus on (prefixes of the input graph). With a general graph, however, there is no intrinsic ordering of the vertices or edges, and few clues about which subgraphs are the relevant ones.

---

[7]This is equivalent to the *Pigeonhole Principle*: No matter how you stuff $n+1$ pigeons into n holes, there will be a hole with at least two pigeons.

[8]This algorithm was discovered independently by many different people in the mid-to-late 1950s, including Richard E. Bellman and Lester R. Ford, Jr., though ironically Alfonso Shimbel appears to have been the first. History buffs should check out the paper "On the History of the Shortest Path Problem," by Alexander Schrijver (*Documenta Mathematica*, 2012).

The Bellman-Ford algorithm takes a different tack, one inspired by the inherently sequential nature of the *output* of the single-source shortest path problem (i.e., of paths). Intuitively, you might expect that a prefix P' of a shortest path P would itself be a shortest path, albeit to a different destination:

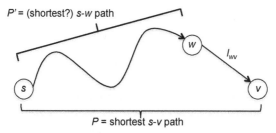

$P' = $ (shortest?) s-w path

$P = $ shortest s-v path

Yet even assuming that this is true (which it is, as we'll see), in what sense is the prefix P' solving a "smaller" subproblem than the original path P? With negative edge lengths, the length of P' might even be larger than that of P. What we do know is that P' contains fewer *edges* than P, which motivates the inspired idea behind the Bellman-Ford algorithm: Introduce a hop count parameter i that artificially restricts the number of edges allowed in a path, with "bigger" subproblems having larger edge budgets i. Then, a path prefix can indeed be viewed as a solution to a smaller subproblem.

For example, consider the graph

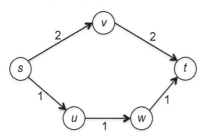

and, for the destination t, the subproblems corresponding to successive values of the edge budget i. When i is 0 or 1, there are no s-t paths with i edges or less, and no solutions to the corresponding subproblems. The shortest-path distance subject to the hop count constraint is effectively $+\infty$. When i is 2, there is a unique s-t path with at most i edges ($s \to v \to t$), and the value of the subproblem is 4. If we bump up i to 3 (or more), the path $s \to u \to w \to t$ becomes eligible and lowers the shortest-path distance from 4 to 3.

Bellman-Ford Algorithm: Subproblems

Compute $L_{i,v}$, the length of a shortest path with at most i edges from s to v in G, with cycles allowed. (If no such path exists, define $L_{i,v}$ as $+\infty$.)

(For each $i \in \{0, 1, 2, \ldots\}$ and $v \in V$.)

Paths with cycles are allowed as solutions to a subproblem. If a path uses an edge multiple times, each use counts against its hop count budget. An optimal solution might well traverse a negative cycle over and over, but eventually it will exhaust its (finite) edge budget. For a fixed destination v, the set of allowable paths grows with i, and so $L_{i,v}$ can only decrease as i increases.

Unlike our previous dynamic programming case studies, every subproblem works with the full input (rather than a prefix or subset of it); the genius of these subproblems lies in how they control the allowable size of the output.

As stated, the parameter i could be an arbitrarily large positive integer and there is an infinite number of subproblems. The solution to Quiz 18.1 hints that perhaps not all of them are important. Shortly, we'll see that there's no reason to bother with subproblems in which i is greater than n, the number of vertices, which implies that there are $O(n^2)$ relevant subproblems.[9]

18.2.2   Optimal Substructure

With our clever choice of subproblems in hand, we can study how optimal solutions must be built up from optimal solutions to smaller subproblems. Consider an input graph $G = (V, E)$ with source vertex $s \in V$, and fix a subproblem, which is defined by a destination vertex $v \in V$ and a hop count constraint $i \in \{1, 2, 3, \ldots\}$. Suppose P is an s-v path with at most i edges, and moreover is a shortest such path. What must it look like? If P doesn't even bother to use up its edge budget, the answer is easy.

---

[9]If this seems like a lot of subproblems, don't forget that the single-source shortest path problem is really n different problems in one (with one problem per destination vertex). There's only a linear number of subproblems per value in the output, which is as good or better than all our other dynamic programming algorithms.

Case 1: P has $i-1$ or fewer edges.   In this case, the path P can immediately be interpreted as a solution to the smaller subproblem with edge budget $i-1$ (still with destination v). The path P must be an optimal solution to this smaller subproblem, as any shorter s-v path with at most $i-1$ edges would also be a superior solution to the original subproblem, contradicting the purported optimality of P.

If the path P uses its full edge budget, we follow the pattern of several previous case studies and pluck off the last edge of P to obtain a solution to a smaller subproblem.

Case 2: P has i edges.   Let L denote the length of P. Let P' denote the first $i-1$ edges of P, and (w, v) its final hop:

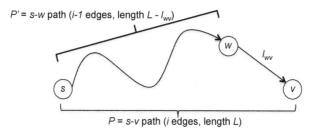

The prefix P' is an s-w path with at most $i-1$ edges and length $L - \ell_{wv}$.[10] There cannot be a shorter such path: If P^* were an s-w path with at most $i-1$ edges and length $L^* < L - \ell_{wv}$, appending the edge (w, v) to P^* would produce an s-v path with at most i edges and length $L^* + \ell_{wv} < (L - \ell_{wv}) + \ell_{wv} = L$, contradicting the optimality of P for the original subproblem.[11]

This case analysis narrows down the possibilities for an optimal solution to a subproblem to a small number of candidates.

Lemma 18.1 (Bellman-Ford Optimal Substructure) *Let $G = (V, E)$ be a directed graph with real-valued edge lengths and source vertex $s \in V$. Suppose $i \geq 1$ and $v \in V$, and let P be a shortest s-v path in G with at most i edges, with cycles allowed. Then, P is either:*

---

[10]The path P' has *exactly* $i-1$ edges. However, we want to establish its superiority to all competing s-w paths with $i-1$ edges *or fewer*.

[11]If P^* already includes the vertex v, adding the edge (w, v) to it creates a cycle; this is not an issue for the proof, as our subproblem definition permits paths with cycles.

(i) a shortest s-v path with at most i − 1 edges; or

(ii) for some w ∈ V, a shortest s-w path with at most i − 1 edges, supplemented with the edge (w, v) ∈ E.

How many candidates, exactly?

Quiz 18.2

How many candidates are there for an optimal solution to a subproblem with the destination v? (Let n denote the number of vertices in the input graph. The in- and out-degree of a vertex is the number of incoming and outgoing edges, respectively.)

  a) 2

  b) 1 + the in-degree of v

  c) 1 + the out-degree of v

  d) n

(See Section 18.2.9 for the solution and discussion.)

18.2.3   Recurrence

As usual, the next step is to compile our understanding of optimal substructure into a recurrence that implements exhaustive search over the possible candidates for an optimal solution. The best of the candidates identified in Lemma 18.1 must be an optimal solution.

Corollary 18.2 (Bellman-Ford Recurrence) *With the assumptions and notation of Lemma 18.1, let $L_{i,v}$ denote the minimum length of an s-v path with at most i edges, with cycles allowed. (If there are no such paths, then $L_{i,v} = +\infty$.) For every $i \geq 1$ and $v \in V$,*

$$L_{i,v} = \min \left\{ \begin{array}{ll} L_{i-1,v} & (Case\ 1) \\ \min_{(w,v)\in E}\{L_{i-1,w} + \ell_{wv}\} & (Case\ 2) \end{array} \right\}. \quad (18.1)$$

The outer "min" in the recurrence implements the exhaustive search over Case 1 and Case 2. The inner "min" implements the exhaustive search inside Case 2 over all possible choices for the final hop of a shortest path. If $L_{i-1,v}$ and all the relevant $L_{i-1,w}$'s are $+\infty$, then v is unreachable from s in i or fewer hops, and we interpret the recurrence as computing $L_{i,v} = +\infty$.

18.2.4   When Should We Stop?

With so much dynamic programming experience now under your belt, your Pavlovian response to the recurrence in Corollary 18.2 might be to write down a dynamic programming algorithm that uses it repeatedly to systematically solve every subproblem. Presumably, the algorithm would start by solving the smallest subproblems (with edge budget $i = 0$), followed by the next-smallest subproblems (with $i = 1$), and so on. One little issue: In the subproblems defined in Section 18.2.1, the edge budget i can be an arbitrarily large positive integer, which means there's an infinite number of subproblems. How do we know when to stop?

A good stopping criterion follows from the observation that the solutions to a given batch of subproblems, with a fixed edge budget i and v ranging over all possible destinations, depend only on the solutions to the previous batch of subproblems (with edge budget $i-1$). Thus, if one batch of subproblems ever has exactly the same optimal solutions as the previous one (with Case 1 of the recurrence winning for every destination), these optimal solutions will remain the same forevermore.

Lemma 18.3 (Bellman-Ford Stopping Criterion) *Under   the assumptions and notation of Corollary 18.2, if for some $k \geq 0$*

$$L_{k+1,v} = L_{k,v} \quad \text{for every destination } v,$$

then:

(a) *$L_{i,v} = L_{k,v}$ for every $i \geq k$ and destination v; and*

(b) *for every destination v, $L_{k,v}$ is the correct shortest-path distance $dist(s,v)$ from s to v in G.*

Proof: By assumption, the input to the recurrence in (18.1) in the $(k + 2)$th batch of subproblems (i.e., the $L_{k+1,v}$'s) is the same as it was for the $(k + 1)$th batch (i.e., the $L_{k,v}$'s). Thus, the output of the recurrence (the $L_{k+2,v}$'s) will also be the same as it was for the previous batch (the $L_{k+1,v}$'s). Repeating this argument as many times as necessary shows that the $L_{i,v}$'s remain the same for all batches $i \geq k$. This proves part (a).

For part (b), suppose for contradiction that $L_{k,v} \neq dist(s, v)$ for some destination v. Because $L_{k,v}$ is the minimum length of an s-v path with at most k hops, there must be an s-v path with $i > k$ hops and length smaller than $L_{k,v}$. But then $L_{i,v} < L_{k,v}$, contradicting part (a) of the lemma. $\mathcal{QED}$

Lemma 18.3 promises that it's safe to stop as soon as subproblem solutions stabilize, with $L_{k+1,v} = L_{k,v}$ for some $k \geq 0$ and all $v \in V$. But will this ever happen? In general, no. *If the input graph has no negative cycles*, however, subproblem solutions are guaranteed to stabilize by the time i reaches n, the number of vertices.

Lemma 18.4 (Bellman-Ford with No Negative Cycles)
Under the assumptions and notation of Corollary 18.2, and also assuming that the input graph G has no negative cycles,

$$L_{n,v} = L_{n-1,v} \quad \text{for every destination } v,$$

where n is the number of vertices in the input graph.

Proof: The solution to Quiz 18.1 implies that, for every destination v, there is a shortest s-v path with at most $n - 1$ edges. In other words, increasing the edge budget i from $n-1$ to n (or to any bigger number) has no effect on the minimum length of an s-v path. $\mathcal{QED}$

Lemma 18.4 shows that if the input graph does not have a negative cycle, subproblem solutions stabilize by the nth batch. Or in contrapositive form: If subproblem solutions *fail* to stabilize by the nth batch, the input graph *does* have a negative cycle.

In tandem, Lemmas 18.3 and 18.4 tell us the last batch of subproblems that we need to bother with: the batch with $i = n$. If subproblem solutions stabilize (with $L_{n,v} = L_{n-1,v}$ for all $v \in V$), Lemma 18.3 implies that the $L_{n-1,v}$'s are the correct shortest-path distances. If subproblem solutions don't stabilize (with $L_{n,v} \neq L_{n-1,v}$ for some $v \in V$), the contrapositive of Lemma 18.4 implies that the input graph G contains a negative cycle, in which case the algorithm is absolved from computing shortest-path distances. (Recall the problem definition in Section 18.1.2.)

18.2.5   Pseudocode

The justifiably famous Bellman-Ford algorithm now writes itself:
Use the recurrence in Corollary 18.2 to systematically solve all the
subproblems, up to an edge budget of $i = n$.

```
Bellman-Ford
```

Input: directed graph $G = (V, E)$ in adjacency-list
representation, a source vertex $s \in V$, and a
real-valued length ℓ_e for each $e \in E$.
Output: $dist(s, v)$ for every vertex $v \in V$, or a
declaration that G contains a negative cycle.

```
// subproblems (i indexed from 0, v indexes V)
```
$A := (n + 1) \times n$ two-dimensional array
```
// base cases (i = 0)
```
$A[0][s] := 0$
for each $v \neq s$ **do**
$\quad A[0][v] := +\infty$
```
// systematically solve all subproblems
```
for $i = 1$ to n **do**   `// subproblem size`
$\quad$ stable $:=$ TRUE   `// for early stopping`
$\quad$ **for** $v \in V$ **do**
$\qquad$ `// use recurrence from Corollary 18.2`
$\qquad A[i][v] :=$
$\qquad \min\{\underbrace{A[i-1][v]}_{\text{Case 1}}, \underbrace{\min_{(w,v) \in E}\{A[i-1][w] + \ell_{wv}\}}_{\text{Case 2}}\}$
$\qquad$ **if** $A[i][v] \neq A[i-1][v]$ **then**
$\qquad\qquad$ stable $:=$ FALSE
$\quad$ **if** stable $=$ TRUE **then**   `// done by Lemma 18.3`
$\qquad$ **return** $\{A[i-1][v]\}_{v \in V}$
```
// failed to stabilize in n iterations
```
return "negative cycle"   `// correct by Lemma 18.4`

The double for loop reflects the two parameters used to define subproblems, the edge budget i and the destination vertex v. By the
time a loop iteration must compute the subproblem solution $A[i][v]$,
all values of the form $A[i-1][v]$ or $A[i-1][w]$ have already been

computed in the previous iteration of the outer for loop (or in the base cases) and are ready and waiting to be looked up in constant time.

Induction (on i) shows that the `Bellman-Ford` algorithm solves every subproblem correctly, with $A[i][v]$ assigned the correct value $L_{i,v}$; the recurrence in Corollary 18.2 justifies the inductive step. If subproblem solutions stabilize, the algorithm returns the correct shortest-path distances (by Lemma 18.3). If not, the algorithm correctly declares that the input graph contains a negative cycle (by Lemma 18.4).

18.2.6 Example

For an example of the `Bellman-Ford` algorithm in action, consider the following input graph:

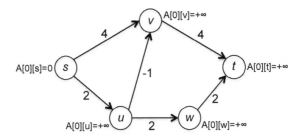

The vertices are labeled with the solutions to the first batch of subproblems (with $i = 0$).

Each iteration of the algorithm evaluates the recurrence (18.1) at each vertex, using the values computed in the previous iteration. In the first iteration, the recurrence evaluates to 0 at s (s has no incoming edges, so Case 2 of the recurrence is vacuous); to 2 at u (because $A[0][s] + \ell_{su} = 2$); to 4 at v (because $A[0][s] + \ell_{sv} = 4$); and to $+\infty$ at w and t (because $A[0][u]$ and $A[0][v]$ are both $+\infty$):

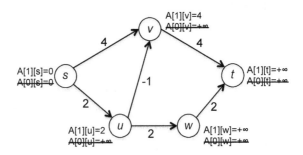

In the next iteration, both s and u inherit solutions from the previous iteration. The value at v drops from 4 (corresponding to the one-hop path $s \to v$) to 1 (corresponding to the two-hop path $s \to u \to v$). The new values at w and t are 4 (because $A[1][u] + \ell_{uw} = 4$) and 8 (because $A[1][v] + \ell_{vt} = 8$):

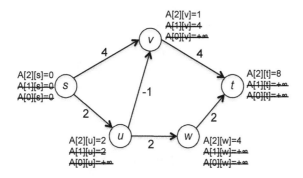

Note that the decrease in shortest-path distance to v in this iteration does not propagate to t immediately, only in the next iteration.

In the third iteration, the value at t drops to 5 (because $A[2][v] + \ell_{vt} = 5$, which is better than both $A[2][t] = 8$ and $A[2][w] + \ell_{wt} = 6$) and the other four vertices inherit solutions from the previous iteration:

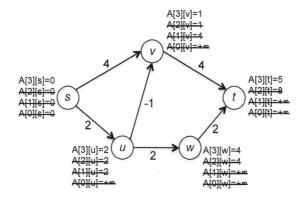

Nothing changes in the fourth iteration:

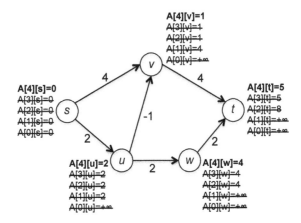

and at this point the algorithm halts with the correct shortest-path distances.[12]

18.2.7   Running Time

The running time analysis of the `Bellman-Ford` algorithm is more interesting than those of our other dynamic programming algorithms.

Quiz 18.3

What's the running time of the `Bellman-Ford` algorithm, as a function of m (the number of edges) and n (the number of vertices)? (Choose the strongest true statement.)

a) $O(n^2)$

b) $O(mn)$

c) $O(n^3)$

d) $O(mn^2)$

(See Section 18.2.9 for the solution and discussion.)

Summarizing everything we now know about the `Bellman-Ford` algorithm:

---

[12]For an example of the algorithm in action on an input graph with a negative cycle, see Problem 18.1.

Theorem 18.5 (Properties of Bellman-Ford) *For every input graph $G = (V, E)$ with n vertices, m edges, real-valued edge lengths, and a source vertex s, the* Bellman-Ford *algorithm runs in $O(mn)$ time and either:*

(i) *returns the shortest-path distance from s to every destination $v \in V$; or*

(ii) *detects that G contains a negative cycle.*

As usual, shortest paths can be reconstructed by tracing back through the final array A computed by the Bellman-Ford algorithm.[13]

18.2.8   Internet Routing

The Bellman-Ford algorithm solves a more general problem than Dijkstra's algorithm (because it accommodates negative edge lengths). Its second advantage is that it is more "distributed" than Dijkstra's algorithm, and for this reason has played the more prominent role in the evolution of Internet routing protocols.[14] Evaluating the recurrence (18.1) at a vertex v requires information only about vertices directly connected to v: the vertices w with an edge (w, v). This suggests that the Bellman-Ford algorithm might be implementable even at an Internet scale, with each machine communicating only with its immediate neighbors and performing only local computations, blissfully unaware of what's going on in the rest of the network. Indeed, the Bellman-Ford algorithm directly inspired the early Inter-

---

[13] For reconstruction purposes, it's a good idea to add one line of code that caches with each vertex v the most recent predecessor w that triggered a Case 2-update of the form $A[i][v] := A[i-1][w] + \ell_{wv}$. (For example, with the input graph in Section 18.2.6, the vertex v's predecessor would be initialized to null, reset to s after the first iteration, and reset again to u after the second iteration.) You can then reconstruct a shortest s-v path backward in $O(n)$ time using the final batch of predecessors by starting from v and following the predecessor trail back to s. As a bonus, because each batch of subproblem solutions and predecessors depends only on those from the previous batch, both the forward and reconstruction passes require only $O(n)$ space (analogous to Problem 17.5). See the bonus video at www.algorithmsilluminated.org for more details.

[14] The Bellman-Ford algorithm was discovered long before the Internet was a gleam in anyone's eye—over 10 years before the ARPANET, which was the earliest precursor to the Internet.

net routing protocols RIP and RIP2—yet another example of how algorithms shape the world as we know it.[15]

18.2.9   Solutions to Quizzes 18.2–18.3

Solution to Quiz 18.2

Correct answer: (b). The optimal substructure lemma (Lemma 18.1) is stated as if there were two candidates for an optimal solution, but Case 2 comprises several subcases, one for each possible final hop (w, v) of an s-v path. The possible final hops are the incoming edges at v. Thus, Case 1 contributes one candidate and Case 2 a number of candidates equal to the in-degree of v. This in-degree could be as large as $n - 1$ in a directed graph (with no parallel edges), but is generally much smaller, especially in sparse graphs.

Solution to Quiz 18.3

Correct answer: (b). The `Bellman-Ford` algorithm solves $(n + 1) \cdot n = O(n^2)$ different subproblems, where n is the number of vertices. *If* the algorithm performed only a constant amount of work per subproblem (like in all our previous dynamic programming algorithms aside from `OptBST`), the running time of the algorithm would also be $O(n^2)$. But solving a subproblem for a destination v boils down to computing the recurrence in Corollary 18.2 which, by Quiz 18.2, involves exhaustive search through $1 + \text{in-deg}(v)$ candidates, where in-deg(v) is the number of incoming edges at v.[16] Because the in-degree of a vertex could be as large as $n - 1$, this would seem to give a running time bound of $O(n)$ per-subproblem, for an overall running time bound of $O(n^3)$.

---

[15]"RIP" stands for "Routing Information Protocol." If you're looking to nerd out, the nitty-gritty details of the RIP and RIP2 protocols are described in RFCs 1058 and 2453, respectively. ("RFC" stands for "request for comments" and is the primary mechanism by which changes to Internet standards are vetted and communicated.) Bonus videos at www.algorithmsilluminated.org describe some of the engineering challenges involved.

[16]Assuming the input graph is represented using adjacency lists (in particular that an array of incoming edges is associated with each vertex), this exhaustive search can be implemented in time linear in $1 + \text{in-deg}(v)$.

We can do better. Zoom in on a fixed iteration of the outer for loop of the algorithm, with some fixed value of i. The total work performed over all iterations of the inner for loop is proportional to

$$\sum_{v \in V}(1 + \text{in-deg}(v)) = n + \underbrace{\sum_{v \in V}\text{in-deg}(v)}_{=m}.$$

The sum of the in-degrees also goes by a simpler name: m, the number of edges. To see this, imagine removing all the edges from the input graph and adding them back in, one by one. Each new edge adds 1 to the overall edge count, and also adds 1 to the in-degree of exactly one vertex (the head of that edge).

Thus, the total work performed in each of the outer for loop iterations is $O(m+n) = O(m)$.[17] There are at most n such iterations and $O(n)$ work is performed outside the double for loop, leading to an overall running time bound of $O(mn)$. In sparse graphs, where m is linear or near-linear in n, this time bound is much better than the more naive bound of $O(n^3)$.

18.3   The All-Pairs Shortest Path Problem

18.3.1   Problem Definition

Why be content computing shortest-path distances from only a single source vertex? For example, an algorithm for computing driving directions should accommodate any possible origin; this corresponds to the *all-pairs shortest path problem*. We continue to allow negative edge lengths and negative cycles in the input graph.

Problem: All-Pairs Shortest Paths

Input: A directed graph $G = (V, E)$ with n vertices and m edges, and a real-valued length ℓ_e for each edge $e \in E$.

Output: One of the following:

---

[17]Technically, this assumes that m is at least a constant times n, as would be the case if, for example, every vertex v was reachable from the source vertex s. Do you see how to tweak the algorithm to obtain a per-iteration time bound of $O(m)$ without this assumption?

(i) the shortest-path distance $dist(v, w)$ for every ordered
vertex pair $v, w \in V$; or

(ii) a declaration that G contains a negative cycle.

There is no source vertex in the all-pairs shortest path problem. In case (i), the algorithm is responsible for outputting n^2 numbers.[18]

18.3.2   Reduction to Single-Source Shortest Paths

If you're on the lookout for reductions (as you should be; see page 100), you might already see how to apply your ever-growing algorithmic toolbox to the all-pairs shortest path problem. One natural approach is to make repeated use of a subroutine that solves the single-source shortest path problem (like the Bellman-Ford algorithm).

Quiz 18.4

How many invocations of a single-source shortest path subroutine are needed to solve the all-pairs shortest path problem? (As usual, n denotes the number of vertices.)

a) 1

b) $n - 1$

c) n

d) n^2

(See Section 18.3.3 for the solution and discussion.)

Plugging in the Bellman-Ford algorithm (Theorem 18.5) for the single-source shortest path subroutine in Quiz 18.4 gives an $O(mn^2)$-time algorithm for the all-pairs shortest path problem.[19]

---

[18]One important application of algorithms for the all-pairs shortest path problem is to computing the transitive closure of a binary relation. The latter problem is equivalent to the all-pairs reachability problem: Given a directed graph, identify all vertex pairs v, w for which the graph contains at least one v-w path (i.e., for which the hop-count shortest-path distance is finite).

[19]Dijkstra's algorithm can substitute for the Bellman-Ford algorithm if edges' lengths are nonnegative, in which case the running time improves to $O(mn \log n)$.

Can we do better? The running time bound of $O(mn^2)$ is particularly problematic in dense graphs. For example, if $m = \Theta(n^2)$, the running time is *quartic* in n—a running time we haven't seen before and, hopefully, will never see again!

18.3.3   Solution to Quiz 18.4

Correct answer: (c). One invocation of the single-source shortest path subroutine will compute shortest-path distances from a single vertex s to every vertex of the graph (n numbers in all, out of the n^2 required). Invoking the subroutine once for each of the n choices for s computes shortest-path distances for every possible origin and destination.[20]

18.4   The Floyd-Warshall Algorithm

This section solves the all-pairs shortest path problem from scratch and presents our final case study of the dynamic programming algorithm design paradigm. The end result is another selection from the greatest hits compilation, the Floyd-Warshall algorithm.[21]

18.4.1   The Subproblems

Graphs are complex objects. Coming up with the right set of subproblems for a dynamic programming solution to a graph problem can be tricky. The ingenious idea behind the subproblems in the Bellman-Ford algorithm for the single-source shortest path problem (Section 18.2.1) is to always work with the original input graph and impose an artificial constraint on the number of edges allowed in the solution to a subproblem. The edge budget then serves as a measure of subproblem size, and a prefix of an optimal solution to a subproblem can be interpreted as a solution to a smaller subproblem (with the same origin but a different destination).

In sparse graphs (with $m = O(n)$ or close to it), this approaches the best we could hope for (as merely writing down the output already requires quadratic time).

[20]If the input graph has a negative cycle, it will be detected by one of the invocations of the single-source shortest path subroutine.

[21]Named after Robert W. Floyd and Stephen Warshall, but also discovered independently by a number of other researchers in the late 1950s and early 1960s.

The big idea in the Floyd-Warshall algorithm is to go one step further and artificially restrict the *identities of the vertices* that are allowed to appear in a solution. To define the subproblems, consider an input graph $G = (V, E)$ and arbitrarily assign its vertices the names $1, 2, \ldots, n$ (where $n = |V|$). Subproblems are then indexed by prefixes $\{1, 2, \ldots, k\}$ of the vertices, with k serving as the measure of subproblem size, as well as an origin v and destination w.

Floyd-Warshall Algorithm: Subproblems

Compute $L_{k,v,w}$, the minimum length of a path in the input graph G that:

   (i) begins at v;

   (ii) ends at w;

   (iii) uses only vertices from $\{1, 2, \ldots, k\}$ as internal vertices[22]; and

   (iv) does not contain a directed cycle.

(If no such path exists, define $L_{k,v,w}$ as $+\infty$.)

(For each $k \in \{0, 1, 2, \ldots, n\}$ and $v, w \in V$.)

There are $(n + 1) \cdot n \cdot n = O(n^3)$ subproblems, which is a linear number for each of the n^2 values in the output. The batch of largest subproblems (with $k = n$) corresponds to the original problem. For a fixed origin v and destination w, the set of allowable paths grows with k, and so $L_{k,v,w}$ can only decrease as k increases.

For example, consider the graph

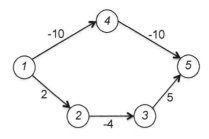

---

[22]Every vertex of a path other than its endpoints is an *internal* vertex.

and, for the origin 1 and the destination 5, the subproblems corresponding to successive values of the prefix length k. When k is 0, 1, or 2, there are no paths from 1 to 5 such that every internal vertex belongs to the prefix $\{1, 2, \ldots, k\}$, and the subproblem's solution is $+\infty$. When $k = 3$, the path $1 \to 2 \to 3 \to 5$ becomes the unique eligible path; it has length $2 + (-4) + 5 = 3$. (The two-hop path is disqualified because it includes vertex 4 as an internal vertex. The three-hop path qualifies even though the vertex 5 does not belong to the prefix $\{1, 2, 3\}$; as the destination, that vertex is granted an exemption.) When $k = 4$ (or larger), the subproblem solution is the length of the true shortest path $1 \to 4 \to 5$, which is -20.

In the next section, we'll see that the payoff of defining subproblems in this way is that there are only two candidates for the optimal solution to a subproblem, depending on whether it makes use of the last allowable vertex k.[23] This leads to a dynamic programming algorithm that performs only $O(1)$ work per subproblem and is therefore faster than n invocations of the Bellman-Ford algorithm (with running time $O(n^3)$ rather than $O(mn^2)$).[24]

18.4.2   Optimal Substructure

Consider an input graph $G = (V, E)$ with vertices labeled 1 to n, and fix a subproblem, defined by an origin vertex v, a destination vertex w, and a prefix length $k \in \{1, 2, \ldots, n\}$. Suppose P is a v-w path with no cycles and all internal vertices in $\{1, 2, \ldots, k\}$, and moreover is a shortest such path. What must it look like? A tautology: The last allowable vertex k either appears as an internal vertex of P, or it doesn't.

Case 1: Vertex k is not an internal vertex of P. In this case, the path P can immediately be interpreted as a solution to a smaller subproblem with prefix length $k - 1$, still with origin v and destination w. The path P must be an optimal solution to the smaller subproblem; any superior solution would also be superior for the original subproblem, a contradiction.

---

[23]By contrast, the number of candidate solutions to a subproblem in the Bellman-Ford algorithm depends on the in-degree of the destination (Quiz 18.2).

[24]Ignore the uninteresting case in which m is much smaller than n; see also footnote 17.

Case 2: Vertex k is an internal vertex of P. In this case, the path P can be interpreted as the amalgamation of *two* solutions to smaller subproblems: the prefix P_1 of P that travels from v to k, and the suffix P_2 of P that travels from k to w.

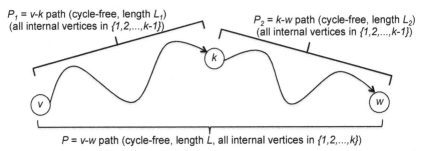

P_1 = v-k path (cycle-free, length L_1) (all internal vertices in {1,2,...,k-1})

P_2 = k-w path (cycle-free, length L_2) (all internal vertices in {1,2,...,k-1})

P = v-w path (cycle-free, length L, all internal vertices in {1,2,...,k})

The vertex k appears in P only once (because P has no cycles) and therefore is not an internal vertex of P_1 or P_2. Thus, we can view P_1 and P_2 as solutions to smaller subproblems, with origins v and k and destinations k and w, respectively, and with all internal vertices in $\{1, 2, \ldots, k-1\}$.[25,26]

You can guess the next step: We want to prove that P_1 and P_2 are, in fact, *optimal* solutions to these smaller subproblems. Let L, L_1, and L_2 denote the lengths of P, P_1, and P_2, respectively. Because P is the union of P_1 and P_2, $L = L_1 + L_2$.

Suppose, for contradiction, that P_1 is not an optimal solution to its subproblem; the argument for P_2 is analogous. Then, there is a cycle-free path P_1^* from v to k with internal vertices in $\{1, 2, \ldots, k-1\}$ and length $L_1^* < L_1$. But then the concatenation of P_1^* and P_2 would be a cycle-free path P^* from v to w with internal vertices in $\{1, 2, \ldots, k\}$ and length $L_1^* + L_2 < L_1 + L_2 = L$, contradicting the assumed optimality of P.

Quiz 18.5

Do you see any bugs in the argument above? (Choose all that apply.)

---

[25]This argument explains why the Floyd-Warshall subproblems, in contrast to the Bellman-Ford subproblems, impose the cycle-free condition (iv).

[26]This approach would *not* work well for the single-source shortest path problem, as the suffix path P_2 would have the wrong origin vertex.

a) The concatenation P^* of P_1^* and P_2 need not have origin v.

b) P^* need not have destination w.

c) P^* need not have internal vertices only in $\{1, 2, \ldots, k\}$.

d) P^* need not be cycle-free.

e) P^* need not have length less than L.

f) Nope, no bugs.

(See Section 18.4.6 for the solution and discussion.)

Is the bug fatal, or do we just need to work a little harder? Suppose the concatenation P^* of P_1^* and P_2 contains a cycle. By repeatedly splicing out cycles (as in Figure 15.2 and footnote 4 in Chapter 15), we can extract from P^* a cycle-free path $\widehat{P}$ with the same origin (v) and destination (w), and with only fewer internal vertices. The length of $\widehat{P}$ equals the length L^* of P^*, less the sum of the lengths of the edges in the spliced-out cycles.

If the input graph has no negative cycles, cycle-splicing can only shorten a path, in which case the length of $\widehat{P}$ is at most L^*. In this case, we've salvaged the proof: $\widehat{P}$ is a cycle-free v-w path with all internal vertices in $\{1, 2, \ldots, k\}$ and length at most $L^* < L$, contradicting the assumed optimality of the original path P. We can then conclude that the vertex k does, indeed, split the optimal solution P into optimal solutions P_1 and P_2 to their respective smaller subproblems.

We're not responsible for computing shortest-path distances for input graphs with a negative cycle. (Recall the problem definition in Section 18.3.) Let's declare victory with the following optimal substructure lemma.

Lemma 18.6 (Floyd-Warshall Optimal Substructure)

Let $G = (V, E)$ be a directed graph with real-valued edge lengths and no negative cycles, with $V = \{1, 2, \ldots, n\}$. Suppose $k \in \{1, 2, \ldots, n\}$ and $v, w \in V$, and let P be a minimum-length cycle-free v-w path in G with all internal vertices in $\{1, 2, \ldots, k\}$. Then, P is either:

(i) a minimum-length cycle-free v-w path with all internal vertices in $\{1, 2, \ldots, k-1\}$; or

(ii) the concatenation of a minimum-length cycle-free v-k path with
all internal vertices in $\{1, 2, \ldots, k-1\}$ and a minimum-length
cycle-free k-w path with all internal vertices in $\{1, 2, \ldots, k-1\}$.

Or, in recurrence form:

Corollary 18.7 (Floyd-Warshall Recurrence) *With the assumptions and notation of Lemma 18.6, let $L_{k,v,w}$ denote the
minimum length of a cycle-free v-w path with all internal vertices
in $\{1, 2, \ldots, k\}$. (If there are no such paths, then $L_{k,v,w} = +\infty$.) For
every $k \in \{1, 2, \ldots, n\}$ and $v, w \in V$,*

$$L_{k,v,w} = \min \left\{ \begin{array}{ll} L_{k-1,v,w} & \text{(Case 1)} \\ L_{k-1,v,k} + L_{k-1,k,w} & \text{(Case 2)} \end{array} \right\}. \qquad (18.2)$$

18.4.3   Pseudocode

Suppose we know that the input graph has no negative cycles, in
which case Lemma 18.6 and Corollary 18.7 apply. We can use the
recurrence to systematically solve all the subproblems, from smallest
to largest. To get started, what are the solutions to the base cases
(with $k = 0$ and no internal vertices are allowed)?

Quiz 18.6

Let $G = (V, E)$ be an input graph. What is $L_{0,v,w}$ in the
case where: (i) $v = w$; (ii) (v, w) is an edge of G; and (iii)
$v \neq w$ and (v, w) is not an edge of G?

a) 0, 0, and $+\infty$

b) 0, ℓ_{vw}, and ℓ_{vw}

c) 0, ℓ_{vw}, and $+\infty$

d) $+\infty$, ℓ_{vw}, and $+\infty$

(See Section 18.4.6 for the solution and discussion.)

The Floyd-Warshall algorithm computes the base cases using
the solution to Quiz 18.6 and the rest of the subproblems using the
recurrence in Corollary 18.7. The final for loop in the pseudocode

checks whether the input graph contains a negative cycle and is explained in Section 18.4.4. See Problems 18.4 and 18.5 for examples of the algorithm in action.

Floyd-Warshall

Input: directed graph $G = (V, E)$ in adjacency-list or adjacency-matrix representation, and a real-valued length ℓ_e for each edge $e \in E$.
Output: $dist(v, w)$ for every vertex pair $v, w \in V$, or a declaration that G contains a negative cycle.

---

label the vertices $V = \{1, 2, \ldots, n\}$ arbitrarily
`// subproblems (k indexed from 0, v,w from 1)`
$A := (n + 1) \times n \times n$ three-dimensional array
`// base cases (k = 0)`
for $v = 1$ **to** n **do**
    for $w = 1$ **to** n **do**
        if $v = w$ **then**
            $A[0][v][w] := 0$
        else if (v, w) is an edge of G **then**
            $A[0][v][w] := \ell_{vw}$
        else
            $A[0][v][w] := +\infty$
`// systematically solve all subproblems`
for $k = 1$ **to** n **do**   `// subproblem size`
    for $v = 1$ **to** n **do**   `// origin`
        for $w = 1$ **to** n **do**   `// destination`
            `// use recurrence from Corollary 18.7`
            $A[k][v][w] :=$
                $\min\{\underbrace{A[k-1][v][w]}_{\text{Case 1}}, \underbrace{A[k-1][v][k] + A[k-1][k][w]}_{\text{Case 2}}\}$

`// check for a negative cycle`
for $v = 1$ **to** n **do**
    if $A[n][v][v] < 0$ **then**
        return "negative cycle"   `// see Lemma 18.8`
return $\{A[n][v][w]\}_{v,w \in V}$

The algorithm uses a three-dimensional array of subproblems and a corresponding triple for loop because subproblems are indexed by three parameters (an origin, a destination, and a prefix of vertices). It's important that the outer loop is indexed by the subproblem size k, so that all of the relevant terms $A[k-1][v][w]$ are available for constant-time look up in each inner loop iteration. (The relative order of the second and third for loops doesn't matter.) There are $O(n^3)$ subproblems and the algorithm performs $O(1)$ work for each one (in addition to $O(n^2)$ work outside the triple for loop), so its running time is $O(n^3)$.[27,28] Induction (on k) and the correctness of the recurrence (Corollary 18.7) imply that, when the input graph has no negative cycle, the algorithm correctly computes the shortest-path distances between each pair of vertices.[29]

18.4.4   Detecting a Negative Cycle

What about when the input graph has a negative cycle? How do we know whether we can trust the solutions to the final batch of subproblems? The "diagonal" entries of the subproblem array are the tell.[30]

Lemma 18.8 (Detecting a Negative Cycle) *The input graph $G = (V, E)$ has a negative cycle if and only if, at the conclusion of the `Floyd-Warshall` algorithm, $A[n][v][v] < 0$ for some vertex $v \in V$.*

Proof: If the input graph does not have a negative cycle, then: (i) `Floyd-Warshall` correctly computes all shortest-path distances; and

---

[27]Unlike most of our graph algorithms, the `Floyd-Warshall` algorithm is equally fast and easy-to-implement for graphs represented with an adjacency matrix (where the (v, w) entry of the matrix is ℓ_{vw} if $(v, w) \in E$ and $+\infty$ otherwise) as for graphs represented with adjacency lists.

[28]Because the solutions to a batch of subproblems depend only on those from the previous batch, the algorithm can be implemented using $O(n^2)$ space (analogous to Problem 17.5).

[29]Had I shown you the Floyd-Warshall algorithm before your boot camp in dynamic programming, your response might have been: "That's an impressively elegant algorithm, but how could I ever have come up with it myself?" Now that you've achieved a black-belt (or at least brown-belt) level of skill in the art of dynamic programming, I hope your reaction is: "How could I *not* have come up with this algorithm myself?"

[30]For a different approach, see Problem 18.6.

(ii) there is no path from a vertex v to itself shorter than the empty path (which has length 0). Thus $A[n][v][v] = 0$ for all $v \in V$ at the end of the algorithm.

To prove the converse, assume that G has a negative cycle. This implies that G has a negative cycle with no repeated vertices other than its start and end. (Do you see why?) Let C denote an arbitrary such cycle. The `Floyd-Warshall` algorithm need not compute the correct shortest-path distances, but it is still the case that $A[k][v][w]$ is *at most* the minimum length of a cycle-free v-w path with internal vertices restricted to $\{1, 2, \ldots, k\}$ (as you should check, by induction on k).

Suppose the vertex k of C has the largest label. Let $v \neq k$ be some other vertex of C:

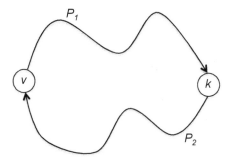

The two sides P_1 and P_2 of the cycle are cycle-free v-k and k-v paths with internal vertices restricted to $\{1, 2, \ldots, k-1\}$, so $A[k-1][v][k]$ and $A[k-1][k][v]$ are at most their respective lengths. Thus $A[k][v][v]$, which is at most $A[k-1][v][k] + A[k-1][k][v]$, is at most the length of the cycle C, which is less than zero. The final value $A[n][v][v]$ can only be smaller. $\mathcal{QED}$

18.4.5   Summary and Open Questions

Summarizing everything we now know about the `Floyd-Warshall` algorithm:

Theorem 18.9 (Properties of `Floyd-Warshall`) *For every input graph $G = (V, E)$ with n vertices and real-valued edge lengths, the `Floyd-Warshall` algorithm runs in $O(n^3)$ time and either:*

(i) returns the shortest-path distances between each pair $v, w \in V$ of vertices; or

(ii) detects that G contains a negative cycle.

As usual, shortest paths can be reconstructed by tracing back through the final array A computed by the Floyd-Warshall algorithm.[31]

How should we feel about the cubic running time of the Floyd-Warshall algorithm? We can't expect a running time better than quadratic (with a quadratic number of values to report), but there's a big gap between cubic and quadratic running times. Can we do better? Nobody knows! One of the biggest open questions in the field of algorithms is whether there is an algorithm for the all-pairs shortest path problem on n-vertex graphs that runs in, say, $O(n^{2.99})$ time.[32]

18.4.6   Solutions to Quizzes 18.5–18.6

Solution to Quiz 18.5

Correct answer: (d). The concatenation P^* of P_1^* and P_2 definitely starts at v (because P_1^* does) and ends at w (because P_2 does). The internal vertices of P^* are the same as those of P_1^* and of P_2, plus the new internal vertex k. Because all of the internal vertices of P_1^* and P_2 belong to $\{1, 2, \ldots, k-1\}$, all of the internal vertices of P^* belong to $\{1, 2, \ldots, k\}$. The length of the concatenation of two paths is the sum of their lengths, so P^* does indeed have length $L_1^* + L_2 < L$.

---

[31]Analogous to the Bellman-Ford algorithm (footnote 13), it's a good idea to maintain with each vertex pair v, w the last hop of a minimum-length cycle-free v-w path with internal vertices restricted to $\{1, 2, \ldots, k\}$. (If Case 1 of the recurrence wins for the vertex pair v, w in the kth batch of subproblems, the last hop for the pair remains the same. If Case 2 wins, the last hop for v, w is reassigned to the most recent last hop for k, w.) Reconstruction for a given vertex pair then requires only $O(n)$ time.

[32]We can do better than the Floyd-Warshall algorithm for graphs that are not very dense. For example, a clever trick reduces the all-pairs shortest path problem (with negative edge lengths) to one invocation of the Bellman-Ford algorithm followed by $n-1$ invocations of Dijkstra's algorithm. This reduction, which is called Johnson's algorithm and described in the bonus videos at www.algorithmsilluminated.org, runs in $O(mn) + (n-1) \cdot O(m \log n) = O(mn \log n)$ time. This is subcubic in n except when m is very close to quadratic in n.

The issue is that the concatenation of two cycle-free paths need not be cycle-free. For example, in the graph

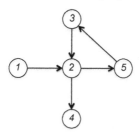

concatenating the path $1 \to 2 \to 5$ with the path $5 \to 3 \to 2 \to 4$ produces a path that contains the directed cycle $2 \to 5 \to 3 \to 2$.

Solution to Quiz 18.6

Correct answer: (c). If $v = w$, the only v-w path with no internal vertices is the empty path (with length 0). If $(v, w) \in E$, the only such path is the one-hop path $v \to w$ (with length ℓ_{vw}). If $v \neq w$ and $(v, w) \notin E$, there are no v-w paths with no internal vertices and $L_{0,v,w} = +\infty$.

The Upshot

☆ It is not obvious how to define shortest-path distances in a graph with a negative cycle.

☆ In the single-source shortest path problem, the input consists of a directed graph with edge lengths and a source vertex. The goal is either to compute the length of a shortest path from the source vertex to every other vertex or to detect that the graph has a negative cycle.

☆ The Bellman-Ford algorithm is a dynamic programming algorithm that solves the single-source shortest path problem in $O(mn)$ time, where m and n are the number of edges and vertices of the input graph, respectively.

☆ The key idea in the Bellman-Ford algorithm is to

parameterize subproblems by an edge budget i (in addition to a destination) and consider only paths with i or fewer edges.

☆ The Bellman-Ford algorithm has played a prominent role in the evolution of Internet routing protocols.

☆ In the all-pairs shortest path problem, the input consists of a directed graph with edge lengths. The goal is to either compute the length of a shortest path from every vertex to every other vertex, or detect that the graph has a negative cycle.

☆ The Floyd-Warshall algorithm is a dynamic programming algorithm that solves the all-pairs shortest path problem in $O(n^3)$ time, where n is the number of vertices of the input graph.

☆ The key idea in the Floyd-Warshall algorithm is to parameterize subproblems by a prefix of k vertices (in addition to an origin and a destination) and consider only cycle-free paths with all internal vertices in $\{1, 2, \ldots, k\}$.

Test Your Understanding

Problem 18.1 *(S)* For the input graph

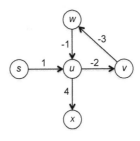

what are the final array entries of the `Bellman-Ford` algorithm from Section 18.2?

Problem 18.2 *(S)* Lemma 18.3 shows that once the subproblem solutions stabilize in the Bellman-Ford algorithm (with $L_{k+1,v} = L_{k,v}$ for every destination v), they remain the same forevermore (with $L_{i,v} = L_{k,v}$ for all $i \geq k$ and $v \in V$). Is this also true on a per-vertex basis? That is, is it true that, whenever $L_{k+1,v} = L_{k,v}$ for some $k \geq 0$ and destination v, $L_{i,v} = L_{k,v}$ for all $i \geq k$? Provide either a proof or a counterexample.

Problem 18.3 *(H)* Consider a directed graph $G = (V, E)$ with n vertices, m edges, a source vertex $s \in V$, real-valued edge lengths, and no negative cycles. Suppose you know that every shortest path in G from s to another vertex has at most k edges. How quickly can you solve the single-source shortest path problem? (Choose the strongest statement that is guaranteed to be true.)

a) $O(m + n)$

b) $O(kn)$

c) $O(km)$

d) $O(mn)$

Problem 18.4 *(S)* For the input graph

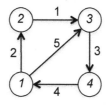

what are the final array entries of the `Floyd-Warshall` algorithm from Section 18.4?

Problem 18.5 *(S)* For the input graph

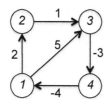

what are the final array entries of the `Floyd-Warshall` algorithm?

Challenge Problems

Problem 18.6 *(S)* The Floyd-Warshall algorithm runs in $O(n^3)$ time on graphs with n vertices and m edges, whether or not the input graph contains a negative cycle. Modify the algorithm so that it solves the all-pairs shortest path problem in $O(mn)$ time for input graphs with a negative cycle and $O(n^3)$ time otherwise.

Problem 18.7 *(H)* Which of the following problems can be solved in $O(n^3)$ time, where n is the number of vertices in the input graph?

a) Given a directed graph $G = (V, E)$ with nonnegative edge lengths, compute the maximum length of a shortest path between any pair of vertices (that is, $\max_{v,w \in V} dist(v, w)$).

b) Given a directed acyclic graph with real-valued edge lengths, compute the length of a longest path between any pair of vertices.

c) Given a directed graph with nonnegative edge lengths, compute the length of a longest cycle-free path between any pair of vertices.

d) Given a directed graph with real-valued edge lengths, compute the length of a longest cycle-free path between any pair of vertices.

Programming Problems

Problem 18.8 Implement in your favorite programming language the Bellman-Ford and Floyd-Warshall algorithms. For the all-pairs shortest path problem, how much faster is the Floyd-Warshall algorithm than n invocations of the Bellman-Ford algorithm? For bonus points, implement the space optimizations and linear-time reconstruction algorithms outlined in footnotes 13, 28, and 31. (See www.algorithmsilluminated.org for test cases and challenge data sets.)

Epilogue: A Field Guide to Algorithm Design

With three parts of the *Algorithms Illuminated* series under your belt, you now possess a rich algorithmic toolbox suitable for tackling a wide range of computational problems. When putting it into practice, you might find the sheer number of algorithms, data structures, and design paradigms daunting. When confronted with a new problem, what's the most effective way to put your tools to work? To give you a starting point, I'll tell you the typical recipe I use when I need to understand a new computational problem. I encourage you to develop your own recipe based on your personal experience.

1. Can you avoid solving the problem from scratch? Is it a disguised version, variant, or special case of a problem that you already know how to solve? For example, can it be reduced to sorting, graph search, or a shortest-path computation?[33] If so, use the fastest algorithm sufficient for solving the problem.

2. Can you simplify the problem by processing the input using a for-free primitive, such as sorting or computing connected components?

3. If you must design a new algorithm from scratch, get calibrated by identifying the line in the sand drawn by the "obvious" solution (such as exhaustive search). Is the running time of the obvious solution already good enough?

4. If the obvious solution is inadequate, brainstorm as many natural greedy algorithms as you can and test them on small examples.

---

[33] If you go on to a deeper study of algorithms, beyond the scope of this book series, you can learn several more problems that show up in disguise all the time. A few examples include the fast Fourier transform, the maximum flow and minimum cut problems, bipartite matching, and linear and convex programming.

Most likely, all will fail. But the ways in which they fail will help you better understand the problem.

5. If there is a natural way to break down the problem into smaller subproblems, how easy would it be to combine their solutions into one for the original problem? If you see how to do it efficiently, proceed with the divide-and-conquer paradigm.

6. Try dynamic programming. Can you argue that a solution must be built up from solutions to smaller subproblems in one of a small number of ways? Can you formulate a recurrence to quickly solve a subproblem given solutions to a modest number of smaller subproblems?

7. In the happy case that you devise a good algorithm for the problem, can you make it even better by deploying the right data structures? Look for significant computations that your algorithm performs over and over again (like lookups or minimum computations). Remember the principle of parsimony: Choose the simplest data structure that supports all the operations required by your algorithm.

8. Can you make your algorithm simpler or faster using randomization? For example, if your algorithm must choose one object among many, what happens when it chooses randomly?

9. (To be covered in *Part 4*.) If all preceding steps end in failure, contemplate the unfortunate but common possibility that there is *no* efficient algorithm for your problem. Can you prove that your problem is computationally intractable by reducing a known NP-hard problem to it?

10. (To be covered in *Part 4*.) Iterate over the algorithm design paradigms again, this time looking for opportunities for fast heuristics (especially with greedy algorithms) and better-than-exhaustive-search exact algorithms (especially with dynamic programming).

Hints and Solutions to Selected Problems

Hint for Problem 13.1: One of the greedy algorithms can be proved correct using an exchange argument, similar to the one in Section 13.4.

Hint for Problem 13.2: For each of the incorrect algorithms, there is a counterexample with only two jobs.

Hint for Problem 13.3: Let S_i denote the set of jobs with the i earliest finish times. Prove by induction on i that your greedy algorithm of choice selects the maximum-possible number of non-conflicting jobs from S_i.

Solution to Problem 14.1: (a). Achieved, for example, by the code

Symbol	Encoding
A	00
B	01
C	10
D	110
E	111

Solution to Problem 14.2: (a). Achieved, for example, by the code

Symbol	Encoding
A	110
B	1110
C	0
D	1111
E	10

Hint for Problem 14.3: For a lower bound, consider symbol frequencies that are powers of 2.

Hint for Problem 14.4: For (c), prove that a letter with frequency less than 0.33 participates in at least one merge prior to the final iteration. For (d), see Problem 14.2.

Solution to Problem 14.5: Sort the symbols by frequency and insert them in increasing order into a queue Q_1.[34] Initialize an empty queue Q_2. Maintain the following invariants: (i) the elements of Q_1 correspond to single-node trees in the current forest $\mathcal{F}$, stored in increasing order of frequency; (ii) the elements of Q_2 correspond to the multi-node trees of $\mathcal{F}$, stored in increasing order of sum of symbol frequencies. In each iteration of the algorithm, the trees T_1 and T_2 with the smallest sums of symbol frequencies can be identified and removed using a constant number of operations at the fronts of Q_1 and Q_2. The merger T_3 of T_1 and T_2 is inserted at the back of Q_2. (Exercise: why does invariant (ii) continue to hold?) Every queue operation (removing from the front or adding to the back) runs in $O(1)$ time, so the total running time of the $n - 1$ iterations of the main loop is $O(n)$.

Hint for Problem 15.1: To reason about T, use Corollary 15.8 or the minimum bottleneck property (page 70). To reason about P, think about two s-t paths with different numbers of edges.

Hint for Problem 15.2: Use Lemma 15.7 to prove that the output is a spanning tree. Prove that every edge that fails to satisfy the minimum bottleneck property (page 70) is excluded from the final output and use Theorem 15.6.

Hint for Problem 15.3: Three of the four problems reduce easily to the MST problem. For one of them, use the fact that $\ln(x \cdot y) = \ln x + \ln y$ for $x, y > 0$.

Solution to Problem 15.4: Suppose an edge $e = (v, w)$ of an MST T of a graph G does not satisfy the minimum bottleneck property and let P denote a v-w path in G in which every edge has cost less

---

[34]If you're unfamiliar with queues, now is a good time to read up on them in your favorite introductory programming book (or on Wikipedia). The gist is that a queue is a data structure for maintaining a list of objects, and you can remove stuff from its front or add stuff to its back in constant time. One way to implement a queue is with a doubly-linked list.

than c_e. Removing e from T creates two connected components, S_1 (containing v) and S_2 (containing w). The v-w path P includes an edge $e' = (x, y)$ with $x \in S_1$ and $y \in S_2$. The edge set $T' = T - \{e\} \cup \{e'\}$ is a spanning tree with total cost less than that of T, contradicting the assumption that T is an MST.

Solution to Problem 15.5: We outline the argument for Kruskal's algorithm; the argument for Prim's algorithm is similar. Let $G = (V, E)$ be a connected undirected graph with real-valued edge costs that need not be distinct. We can assume that not all edges have the same cost, and more generally that not all spanning trees have the same total cost (why?). Let δ_1 denote the smallest strictly positive difference between two edges' costs. Let M^* denote the cost of an MST of G, and M the minimum cost of a suboptimal spanning tree of G. Define δ_2 as $M - M^*$ and $\delta = \min\{\delta_1, \delta_2\} > 0$. Let e_i denote the ith edge of G considered by the `Kruskal` algorithm (after arbitrarily breaking ties in its sorting preprocessing step). Obtain a new graph G' from G by increasing the cost of each edge e_i from c_{e_i} to $c'_{e_i} = c_{e_i} + \delta/2^{(m-i+1)}$, where m is the number of edges. The cost of each spanning tree can only increase, and can increase by at most $\delta \cdot \sum_{i=1}^{m} 2^{(m-i+1)} = \delta \cdot \sum_{i=1}^{m} 2^{-i} < \delta$. Because $\delta \leq \delta_2$, an MST T of G' must also be one of G. Because $\delta \leq \delta_1$, the edges of G' have distinct costs, with edge e_i the ith-cheapest edge of G'. The `Kruskal` algorithm examines the edges of G and G' in the same order, and hence outputs the same spanning tree T^* in both cases. From our proof of correctness of the `Kruskal` algorithm for graphs with distinct edge costs, we know that T^* is an MST of G', and hence of G as well.

Hint for Problem 15.6: Follow the proof of Theorem 15.6.

Solution to Problem 15.7: For (a), suppose for contradiction that there is an MST T that excludes $e = (v, w)$. As a spanning tree, T contains a v-w path P. Because v and w are on different sides of the cut (A, B), P includes an edge e' that crosses (A, B). By assumption, the cost of e' exceeds that of e. Thus $T' = T \cup \{e\} - \{e'\}$ is a spanning tree with cost less than that of T, a contradiction. For (b), every iteration of Prim's algorithm chooses the cheapest edge e that crosses the cut $(X, V - X)$, where X is the set of vertices spanned by the solution-so-far. The Cut Property then implies that every MST contains every edge of the algorithm's final spanning tree T, and so T

is the unique MST. For (c), similarly, every edge chosen by Kruskal's algorithm is justified by the Cut Property. Each edge $e = (v, w)$ added by the algorithm is the cheapest one with endpoints in distinct connected components of the solution-so-far (as these are precisely the edges whose addition will not create a cycle). In particular, e is the cheapest edge crossing the cut (A, B), where A is v's current connected component and $B = V - A$ is everything else.

Hint for Problem 15.8: For (a), the high-level idea is to perform a binary search for the bottleneck of an MBST. Compute the median edge cost in the input graph G. (How do you do this in linear time? See Chapter 6 of *Part 1*.) Obtain G' from G by throwing out all the edges with cost higher than the median. Proceed by recursing on a graph with half as many edges as G. (The easy case is when G' is connected; how do you recurse if G' is not connected?) For the running time analysis, use induction or case 2 of the master method (described in Chapter 4 of *Part 1*).

For (b), the answer appears to be no. (Every MST is an MBST but not conversely, as you should check.) The question of whether there is a deterministic linear-time algorithm for the MST problem remains open to this day; see the bonus video at www.algorithmsilluminated.org for the full story.

Solution to Problem 16.1:

0	5	5	6	12	12	16	18

and the first, fourth, and seventh vertices.

Hint for Problem 16.2: For (a) and (c), revisit the four-vertex example on page 105. For (d), use induction and Lemma 16.1.

Hint for Problem 16.3: If G is a tree, root it at an arbitrary vertex and define one subproblem for each subtree. For an arbitrary graph G, what would your subproblems be?

Solution to Problem 16.4: With columns indexed by i and rows by c:

Hints and Solutions to Selected Problems							207

9	0	1	3	6	8	10
8	0	1	3	6	8	9
7	0	1	3	6	7	9
6	0	1	3	6	6	8
5	0	1	3	5	5	6
4	0	1	3	4	4	5
3	0	1	2	4	4	4
2	0	1	1	3	3	3
1	0	1	1	1	1	1
0	0	0	0	0	0	0
	0	1	2	3	4	5

and the second, third, and fifth items.

Hint for Problem 16.5: For (b) and (c), add a third parameter to the dynamic programming solution to the original knapsack problem in Section 16.5. For (d), how does the generalization of your solution to (c) scale with the number m of knapsacks?

Solution to Problem 17.1: With columns indexed by i and rows by j:

6	6	5	4	5	4	5	4
5	5	4	5	4	3	4	5
4	4	3	4	3	4	5	6
3	3	2	3	4	3	4	5
2	2	1	2	3	4	3	4
1	1	0	1	2	3	4	5
0	0	1	2	3	4	5	6
	0	1	2	3	4	5	6

Hint for Problem 17.2: In each loop iteration, have the necessary subproblem solutions already been computed in previous iterations (or as a base case)?

Solution to Problem 17.3: The problems in (b) and (d) can be solved using algorithms similar to NW, with one subproblem for each pair X_i, Y_j of input string prefixes. Alternatively, the problem in (b) reduces to the sequence alignment problem by setting the gap penalty to 1 and the penalty of matching two different symbols to a very large number.

The problem in (a) can be solved by a generalization of the NW algorithm that keeps track of whether an inserted gap is the first in a sequence of gaps (in which case it carries a penalty of $a + b$) or not (in which case the additional penalty is a). For each pair of prefixes of the input strings, compute the total penalty of three alignments: the best one with no gaps in the final column, the best one with a gap in the upper row of the final column, and the best one with a gap in the lower row of the final column. The number of subproblems and the work-per-subproblem each blow up by a constant factor.

The problem in (c) can be solved efficiently without using dynamic programming; simply count the frequency of each symbol in each string. The permutation f exists if and only if every symbol occurs exactly the same number of times in each string. (Do you see why?)

Solution to Problem 17.4: With columns indexed by i and rows by $j = i + s$:

7	223	158	143	99	74	31	25	0
6	151	105	90	46	26	3	0	
5	142	97	84	40	20	0		
4	92	47	37	10	0			
3	69	27	17	0				
2	30	5	0					
1	20	0						
0	0							
	1	2	3	4	5	6	7	8

Hint for Problem 17.5: The idea is to reuse space once a subproblem solution is rendered irrelevant for future computations. To carry out its entire computation, the WIS algorithm must remember only the two most recent subproblems. The NW algorithm must remember subproblem solutions for the current and preceding values of i, and for all values of j (why?). What about the OptBST algorithm?

Hint for Problem 17.6: Don't bother solving subproblems for prefixes X_i and Y_j with $|i - j| > k$.

Hint for Problem 17.7: The running time of your algorithm should be bounded by a polynomial function of n—a really, really big polynomial!

Solution to Problem 18.1: With columns indexed by i and rows by vertices:

x	$+\infty$	$+\infty$	5	5	5	-1
w	$+\infty$	$+\infty$	$+\infty$	-4	-4	-4
v	$+\infty$	$+\infty$	-1	-1	-1	-7
u	$+\infty$	1	1	1	-5	-5
s	0	0	0	0	0	0
	0	1	2	3	4	5

Solution to Problem 18.2: No. For a counterexample, see the previous problem.

Hint for Problem 18.3: Consider stopping a shortest-path algorithm early.

Solution to Problem 18.4: With columns indexed by k and rows by vertex pairs:

$(1,1)$	0	0	0	0	0
$(1,2)$	2	2	2	2	2
$(1,3)$	5	5	3	3	3
$(1,4)$	$+\infty$	$+\infty$	$+\infty$	6	6
$(2,1)$	$+\infty$	$+\infty$	$+\infty$	$+\infty$	8
$(2,2)$	0	0	0	0	0
$(2,3)$	1	1	1	1	1
$(2,4)$	$+\infty$	$+\infty$	$+\infty$	4	4
$(3,1)$	$+\infty$	$+\infty$	$+\infty$	$+\infty$	7
$(3,2)$	$+\infty$	$+\infty$	$+\infty$	$+\infty$	9
$(3,3)$	0	0	0	0	0
$(3,4)$	3	3	3	3	3
$(4,1)$	4	4	4	4	4
$(4,2)$	$+\infty$	6	6	6	6
$(4,3)$	$+\infty$	9	7	7	7
$(4,4)$	0	0	0	0	0
	0	1	2	3	4

Solution to Problem 18.5: With columns indexed by k and rows by vertex pairs:

$(1,1)$	0	0	0	0	-4
$(1,2)$	2	2	2	2	-2
$(1,3)$	5	5	3	3	-1
$(1,4)$	$+\infty$	$+\infty$	$+\infty$	0	-4
$(2,1)$	$+\infty$	$+\infty$	$+\infty$	$+\infty$	-6
$(2,2)$	0	0	0	0	-4
$(2,3)$	1	1	1	1	-3
$(2,4)$	$+\infty$	$+\infty$	$+\infty$	-2	-6
$(3,1)$	$+\infty$	$+\infty$	$+\infty$	$+\infty$	-7
$(3,2)$	$+\infty$	$+\infty$	$+\infty$	$+\infty$	-5
$(3,3)$	0	0	0	0	-4
$(3,4)$	-3	-3	-3	-3	-7
$(4,1)$	-4	-4	-4	-4	-8
$(4,2)$	$+\infty$	-2	-2	-2	-6
$(4,3)$	$+\infty$	1	-1	-1	-5
$(4,4)$	0	0	0	-4	-8
	0	1	2	3	4

Solution to Problem 18.6: Modify the input graph $G = (V, E)$ by adding a new source vertex s and a new zero-length edge from s to each vertex $v \in V$. The new graph G' has a negative cycle reachable from s if and only if G has a negative cycle. Run the Bellman-Ford algorithm on G' with source vertex s to check whether G contains a negative cycle. If not, run the Floyd-Warshall algorithm on G.

Hint for Problem 18.7: Longest-path problems can be reframed as shortest-path problems after multiplying all edge lengths by -1. Recall from page 170 the problem of computing shortest cycle-free paths in graphs with negative cycles and the fact that it appears to admit no polynomial-time algorithm. Does this fact have any implications for any of the four stated problems?

Index

CPSIA information can be obtained
at www.ICGtesting.com
Printed in the USA
LVHW041122141222
735149LV00002B/187